HELPING CHILDRE

URSULA MARKHAM
therapist, counsellor and st
Her own two children are n
trained by Romark – famou̲ ̲a̲s̲ ̲t̲h̲e̲ ̲T̲V̲ ̲Hypnotherapist
– in his Harley Street clinic. She worked with him for
several years and, since his death in 1982, has had her
own successful practice where she treats patients for
anxiety, depression, lack of confidence, smoking,
phobias, and other common problems. In addition to
running clinics near her home in Gloucestershire,
Ursula Markham frequently lectures and conducts
workshops up and down the country. She is the author of
several books, including *Hypnothink* (Thorsons 1985),
which has been translated into several languages.

Overcoming Common Problems Series

Beating Job Burnout
DR DONALD SCOTT

Beating the Blues
SUSAN TANNER AND JILLIAN BALL

Being the Boss
STEPHEN FITZSIMON

Birth Over Thirty
SHEILA KITZINGER

Body Language
How to read others' thoughts by their gestures
ALLAN PEASE

Bodypower
DR VERNON COLEMAN

Bodysense
DR VERNON COLEMAN

Calm Down
How to cope with frustration and anger
DR PAUL HAUCK

Comfort for Depression
JANET HORWOOD

Common Childhood Illnesses
DR PATRICIA GILBERT

Complete Public Speaker
GYLES BRANDRETH

Coping Successfully with Your Child's Asthma
DR PAUL CARSON

Coping Successfully with Your Child's Skin Problems
DR PAUL CARSON

Coping Successfully with Your Hyperactive Child
DR PAUL CARSON

Coping Successfully with Your Irritable Bowel
ROSEMARY NICOL

Coping with Anxiety and Depression
SHIRLEY TRICKETT

Coping with Cot Death
SARAH MURPHY

Coping with Depression and Elation
DR PATRICK McKEON

Coping with Stress
DR GEORGIA WITKIN-LANOIL

Coping with Suicide
DR DONALD SCOTT

Coping with Thrush
CAROLINE CLAYTON

Curing Arthritis – The Drug-Free Way
MARGARET HILLS

Curing Arthritis Diet Book
MARGARET HILLS

Curing Coughs, Colds and Flu – The Drug-Free Way
MARGARET HILLS

Curing Illness – The Drug-Free Way
MARGARET HILLS

Depression
DR PAUL HAUCK

Divorce and Separation
ANGELA WILLANS

The Dr Moerman Cancer Diet
RUTH JOCHEMS

The Epilepsy Handbook
SHELAGH McGOVERN

Everything You Need to Know about Adoption
MAGGIE JONES

Everything You Need to Know about Contact Lenses
DR ROBERT YOUNGSON

Everything You Need to Know about Osteoporosis
ROSEMARY NICOL

Everything You Need to Know about Shingles
DR ROBERT YOUNGSON

Everything You Need to Know about Your Eyes
DR ROBERT YOUNGSON

Family First Aid and Emergency Handbook
DR ANDREW STANWAY

Overcoming Common Problems Series

Feverfew
A traditional herbal remedy for migraine
and arthritis
DR STEWART JOHNSON

Fight Your Phobia and Win
DAVID LEWIS

Getting Along with People
DIANNE DOUBTFIRE

Goodbye Backache
DR DAVID IMRIE WITH COLLEEN
DIMSON

Helping Children Cope with Divorce
ROSEMARY WELLS

Helping Children Cope with Grief
ROSEMARY WELLS

How to be a Successful Secretary
SUE DYSON AND STEPHEN HOARE

How to Be Your Own Best Friend
DR PAUL HAUCK

How to Control your Drinking
DRS W. MILLER AND R. MUNOZ

How to Cope with Stress
DR PETER TYRER

**How to Cope with Tinnitus and Hearing
Loss**
DR ROBERT YOUNGSON

How to Cope with Your Child's Allergies
DR PAUL CARSON

How to Cure Your Ulcer
ANNE CHARLISH AND DR BRIAN
GAZZARD

How to Do What You Want to Do
DR PAUL HAUCK

How to Enjoy Your Old Age
DR B. F. SKINNER AND M. E.
VAUGHAN

How to Get Things Done
ALISON HARDINGHAM

How to Improve Your Confidence
DR KENNETH HAMBLY

How to Interview and Be Interviewed
MICHELE BROWN AND GYLES
BRANDRETH

How to Love a Difficult Man
NANCY GOOD

How to Love and be Loved
DR PAUL HAUCK

How to Make Successful Decisions
ALISON HARDINGHAM

How to Move House Successfully
ANNE CHARLISH

How to Pass Your Driving Test
DONALD RIDLAND

How to Say No to Alcohol
KEITH McNEILL

How to Spot Your Child's Potential
CECILE DROUIN AND ALAIN DUBOS

How to Stand up for Yourself
DR PAUL HAUCK

**How to Start a Conversation and Make
Friends**
DON GABOR

How to Stop Feeling Guilty
DR VERNON COLEMAN

How to Stop Smoking
GEORGE TARGET

How to Stop Taking Tranquillisers
DR PETER TYRER

How to Stop Worrying
DR FRANK TALLIS

Hysterectomy
SUZIE HAYMAN

If Your Child is Diabetic
JOANNE ELLIOTT

Jealousy
DR PAUL HAUCK

Learning to Live with Multiple Sclerosis
DR ROBERT POVEY, ROBIN DOWIE
AND GILLIAN PRETT

Overcoming Common Problems Series

Overcoming Common Problems

HELPING CHILDREN COPE
WITH STRESS

Ursula Markham

SHELDON PRESS
LONDON

First published in Great Britain in 1990
Sheldon Press, SPCK, Marylebone Road, London NW1 4DU

British Library Cataloguing in Publication Data
Markham, Ursula
 Helping Children Cope with Stress. – (Overcoming common problems)
 1. Children. Stress
 I. Title   II. Series
 155.4

 ISBN 0–85969–608–1

Typeset by Deltatype Ltd, Ellesmere Port, Cheshire
Printed in Great Britain by Biddles Ltd, Guildford and Kings Lynn

To Philip and David
with all my love

The little world of childhood with its familiar surroundings is a model of the greater world. The more intensively the family has shaped its character upon the child, the more it will tend to feel and see its earlier miniature world again in the bigger world of adult life.

C. G. JUNG
Psychological Reflections

Contents

Introduction

The amount of pressure felt by all of us today is far greater than it has ever been before. This is reflected in all levels of society and in every age group. The pensioner, apart from coping with the natural anxieties that accompany the advancing years, also has to manage on sums that may have seemed generous when provision was made so long ago but which now seem pitifully inadequate. The working man or woman has to contend with the combined stresses of job, home and finance. The young couple must face the problems of setting up home, deciding when and if to have a family, and often a conflict of careers. The school-leaver has to compete in a world where regular employment can no longer be taken for granted.

But nowhere is the increase in the amount of stress felt more dramatically than in the lives of children. And nowhere is it more vital to do something about that situation before it gets any worse. Apart from the fact that the results of such stress can make the child's present life miserable, if nothing is done about it the anxious child of today will become the unhappy adult of tomorrow, beset by all the problems anxiety brings – from the inability to form stable relationships to the many serious and even life-threatening health conditions that have now been shown to be predominantly stress-induced.

Yet it is here, among the children, that dramatic changes can be made. We, the adults, have it in our power to help our children deal with the stresses of their young lives, so that they may learn to eliminate some and to cope with those which are unavoidable without having to suffer long-lasting ill effects.

This book is divided into three separate sections, each section having a separate purpose, although naturally all are interlinked.

Part I is designed to help you identify signs and symptoms of stress in your child. After all, if you do not know that such stress exists, how can you help the child to overcome it?

Part II deals with the most common reasons for the onset of stress in children, explaining how it is caused and what you – the caring adult – can do to help ease the situation.

Part III contains advice on general 'stress-proofing'. You cannot safeguard your child from all pressures and anxieties in life but you can do your best to make sure that he or she is as resilient as possible so that the effects of those pressures and anxieties will cause the minimum of suffering.

None of the methods or techniques described in Part III are in any way extreme. Most constitute a slight adjustment to normal, everyday life. All are simple to understand and put into practice. But they can be responsible for changing the whole course of your child's future for the better.

PART ONE
How To Identify Stress In Your Child

1

Identifying Stress

Before you can deal with any problem, you have to recognize that it exists – and this is where the difficulty so often lies. It is not always easy to identify signs of stress in a child and so the situation often goes unnoticed until it has escalated out of all proportion.

An adult will usually tell you if he or she is suffering from a stress-induced illness – although, of course, they may not necessarily recognize it as such. They may simply realize that they are not sleeping as well as usual, that they are getting too many headaches lately or that their doctor has told them to watch their blood pressure. But he or she will tell you *something*. A child often does not realize – and even more often will not tell you – that anything is amiss. So it is up to the parent or other caring adult to look out for tell-tale signs and symptoms of stress in the child.

This section of the book is designed to help you to do just that: to identify signs of stress or distress in your child and to discover where possible the sources of that stress, so that you may be better able to deal with it. What follows is a selection of the most common symptoms of stress and anxiety in a child, but do remember that what you are looking for is a repeated pattern and not just an isolated instance, which may well have no real significance.

Changes in behaviour

Naturally we are not talking here about the normally placid little girl whose temper is aroused when she sees someone throwing stones at a cat or taking toys from her baby brother. Such spontaneous reactions are both usual and understandable. Changes of significance are more permanent, although they may well have come about gradually and you might not even notice them until they have been around for some time.

Aggression

A certain amount of aggression is normal and natural in a very young child, although hopefully as the child grows it will be possible

5

to change that instinctive reaction from aggression to assertion. After all, the child who is assertive will be able to stand up for him or herself and is unlikely to become one of life's 'yes-men'.

A baby or very young child will often have no other way of expressing its frustrations than by screaming in temper. But should an older child begin to show signs of violence or destruction towards themselves and their property or towards others, then that aggression should be taken as a probable symptom of underlying stress.

Sally's mother was completely taken aback when the teacher asked to see her to discuss her eight-year-old daughter's behaviour towards the other children. It seemed that Sally had become violent and aggressive towards the others in her class, pinching, scratching and kicking in what appeared to be unprovoked attacks. Naturally this had resulted in complete isolation for the girl as none of the other children wanted anything to do with her. Her mother could hardly believe that this was the same child who was so quiet and well-behaved at home. On looking into the matter further, it was found that Sally, an only child, was often the centre of attention among the adoring adult members of the family and she was becoming less and less able to cope with being 'one of the crowd' in the school environment. If the only way to be noticed was for antisocial behaviour, then that was how she was going to behave. At home, however, where there was still no competition, this behaviour was unnecessary.

Naturally, more is needed to repair the situation than mere identification of its existence and cause, but that identification is absolutely essential as without it one would merely be dealing with the symptom (in this case the bullying behaviour) and not with the underlying problem. Once she had realized the reason for her daughter's behaviour in school, Sally's mother was able to help her adjust gradually by allowing her to invite other children to the house and on family outings, and by taking her to dancing classes, Brownies and other activities where she would be mixing with her contemporaries. At the same time she was able to reassure her little girl that she was just as precious and important to the family as she had always been.

Aggressive behaviour can show itself in many ways. A child may well become violent or destructive towards property – either their own or other people's. Sometimes they will openly break a toy or tear a book, particularly if the items are their own and even more if the violence is directed towards their favourite possessions. When dealing with items belonging to others, however, the destruction will often be secretly carried out.

Although bullying, unpleasant as it may seem, can usually be dealt with satisfactorily with love and care, symptoms of violence in a child which are directed towards himself often require more expert help. Head-banging or the infliction of physical pain on oneself are often symptoms of a far deeper problem and professional help should *always* be sought in such cases.

Tearfulness

Most children will cry if hurt or if something sad occurs, but the child who seems to cry often and for no apparent reason may well be anxious or suffering from stress. There is little point in telling them not to be a 'cry-baby' or even in pointing out that what appears to be the reason for the tears is something comparatively minor and unimportant. He or she is not even likely to know just why they *are* crying – merely that they cannot help doing so.

Breath-holding

This, of course, is a wonderful way of ensuring that he or she is the centre of attention. From the very first time they observe the results of this action upon the adults around them, the child has a powerful weapon in his or her hands. But, distressing as it may be to see the young face turning purple as they hold their breath, they are not going to do themselves any real physical harm. No-one ever killed themselves by holding their breath – just try it! Breathing is something over which we do not have total control. It is very rare indeed for a loss of consciousness to result but, should it do so, it is not a symptom of stress at all but of a completely different problem and a doctor should be consulted. In most cases, however, the child holding his or her breath is demonstrating their power over those around them. The way to treat such a display is not to try and reason with them while they are in that condition but to feign indifference, and simply walk away. If they wish to shout, scream or cry – or even to run after you – they will have to draw breath to do so.

Change in sleeping habits

Five-year-old Mark, who had slept alone in his own bedroom from the time he was brought home from the hospital at six days old, suddenly developed fears about going to bed. He would beg and plead to be allowed to stay up; he would prolong the whole process of getting undressed and into bed; he would do anything he could to persuade one of his parents to stay with him and, even after the light had finally been switched off, he would call them time after time asking for drinks or saying that he could hear strange noises. Occasionally he would even appear at the sitting-room door complaining that he could not go to sleep.

When a child who has never before had a sleeping problem suddenly develops one, there is always a reason. Most children, particularly the older ones, will do their best to be allowed to stay up a little later but this is normal and nothing to do with fear of going to bed. Mark's parents tried everything they could think of. They left his bedroom door open a little way so that the light from the landing shone into his room; they made sure that, although he had plenty of exercise during the day, Mark had a quiet period before going to bed so that he would be as calm and relaxed as possible. They tried asking Mark why he did not want to go to bed – but unfortunately they usually did this after he had become distressed and so he was unable to give them any coherent answer. Then one day, when Mark was sitting with his mother in the big armchair, he asked her: 'Mummy, what will happen if Sandy wakes up again and he's under the ground?'

Sandy was the pet hamster of Mark's class at school and he had unfortunately died some three weeks earlier. The teacher had explained the situation to the children and told them that Sandy would be buried in a special place in the school grounds. Mark had looked at the little creature whose eyes were, of course, tightly closed – just as if he were asleep. From that moment on sleep and death had become linked in his young mind and he had spent the previous three weeks trying desperately to stay awake so that he would not die and be buried in the ground.

Once she understood the situation, Mark's mother was of course able to explain to him in simple terms the difference between sleep and death and to reassure him that he would not die if he merely closed his eyes and went to sleep. You can see, however, how a lack

8

of understanding that was no-one's fault could lead to anxiety and stress in a young child.

Other bedtime stress symptoms include recurring nightmares (and the subject matter of the nightmare does not necessarily give any indication of the original cause of the stress), fear of the dark, or even the fear his or her parents will go away and leave them while they are alone in bed. No amount of scolding will have any effect in such circumstances, as it is the child's basic insecurity that needs to be treated. If they really are not tired, perhaps you could consider allowing them to go to bed a little later – you will soon be able to see whether they start finding it difficult to get up in the mornings. Perhaps you could allow them to read for a short time before settling down to sleep (preferably something not too horrific). Perhaps they really would be happier with a gentle light in their room until the fears have disappeared.

Changes in eating habits

In children, as in adults, dramatic changes in eating habits are often clear indications of anxiety. This has nothing to do with personal food preferences but with the amount of food eaten. Because excessive over-eating or a sudden inability to eat can have physical causes as well as emotional ones, it is as well for the child to be examined by his doctor to see whether there is a medical reason for the change in pattern. If this is ruled out, however, it is very likely that the child is suffering from stress in some way.

Fears and Phobias

No-one expects a young child to be completely fearless; indeed they would probably be a danger to themselves and to others if they were. But, in a child who is anxious, fear can become a major part of life. Natural nervousness at new experiences is quite normal: the first time he or she jumps into the swimming pool, for example, or when they first ride a bicycle without stabilizers. But constant fears and apprehensions should be taken as a sign that there is some underlying insecurity in the children themselves.

The following are some of the more common fears which are indicative of an accumulation of stress in a child.

Being abandoned

Perhaps he or she has read or seen on television something about an abandoned baby or child. Even fairy tales can put the idea into their mind – think of Hansel and Gretel abandoned in the forest.

It is vitally important for the child's continuing security that you never make threats that will lead them to think that you would abandon them. It is not so long ago that frustrated mothers would warn their offspring about the 'wicked policeman' or the 'bogey-man' who would come to take them away if they did not mend their ways. Only recently one of my patients, whom I shall call Susie, told me that if she misbehaved when she was little (and she is only in her thirties now) her mother would actually pack her suitcase and tell her that she was going to send her to the 'bad children's home'. No wonder that, for the next twenty-five years, Susie suffered from feelings of insecurity and a complete lack of self-confidence!

Fear of going to bed

There can be many causes of bedtime fears in addition to the death/sleep connection.

Young Gavin had never had any bedtime problems until the summer of his sixth birthday, when he suddenly started to play up, even throwing tantrums in order to be allowed to stay up late. Because this behaviour was completely out of character, Gavin's parents spent a long time talking gently to their son in an attempt to discover the cause of the problem. Eventually he was able to explain to them that, because it was light when he went to bed and light when he had to get up, he often did not know which time of day it was. He was not sure whether he had in fact been to sleep and it was now morning or whether he had simply been lying there a short time and it had not yet grown dark. Even the footsteps on the path could have belonged either to his father returning from work or to the postman making an early delivery. Gavin felt completely disorientated and this was why he had tried so hard to be allowed to stay up until it grew dark. That way he would know precisely where he was.

Gavin's parents solved this particular problem by giving the child an alarm clock set for the time he was supposed to get up in the morning. This simple remedy removed all the doubt and insecurity from the child's mind and he was quite happy to go to bed at his usual time once more.

Some children will begin to have frightening dreams or nightmares. Some gentle questioning will soon help you to find out whether or not these are related to problems in their everyday life. This is not always the case, however, as a child has an extremely lively imagination and bad dreams may be the result of something they have read in a book or seen on television.

When Robert was only four he began to have a series of nightmares and, as is often the case, these were all very similar in nature. He would dream of wolves who were chasing either him or members of his family. One night he woke screaming in terror and insisted to his anxious parents that he could hear a wolf scratching on his window as it tried to enter his bedroom. During the day Robert would listen calmly to his mother's assurance that there were no wolves roaming around the south of England where they lived and that nothing could climb up the outside wall of the house to make noises at his window. But at night the fears returned. It was only when his parents found their son looking at a book of fairytales given to him by a fond aunt that they realized that the illustration for 'Red Riding Hood' showed a close-up of the wolf's head, complete with yellow eyes and dripping fangs. Then they discovered that the children at Robert's nursery school had recently been told the story of 'Peter and the Wolf' and also the cautionary tale of 'The Boy who cried "Wolf" '. The combination of all these wolves had just been too much for young Robert and his fertile imagination had brought about the repeated nightmares. Once they understood the cause of the problem, the child's parents and his teacher were all able to reassure him about the local wolf situation – and the offending book was hastily removed.

Of course it is quite possible that a child may simply be trying to test your authority by using any means they can think of to stay up later. Once they discover your vulnerable area you can be sure they will do their best to exploit it. So do not allow yourself to give in to this sort of emotional blackmail.

It is quite a good idea to establish a regular bedtime routine so that, even on a subconscious level, the child's mind is prepared for bed and sleep. However energetic and active he or she may be during the day, try to ensure that the hour before bedtime is fairly quiet. Perhaps – depending upon their age and ability – they can either read or have a story read to them. Perhaps he or she could sit and watch television before having a warm bath and going to bed. But all this will be to no avail if the book or the television programme are exciting or stimulating adventure stories, or if they contain elements of fear and horror. So it may be that a little judicious selection on your part will be necessary.

Fear of doctors, dentists or hospitals

No child is born with a fear of doctors or dentists but unfortunately the first experience many children remember of a doctor's surgery is of the pain of an injection or inoculation. It is not just the pain itself that is significant but the inner feeling of a betrayal of trust. Imagine the scene: a young child is taken by his or her mother to visit the doctor. This nice man or woman talks kindly to them while their mother lifts up their sleeve or gently persuades them to extend their arm. All at once nothing is nice any more. A sharp needle is stuck into their arm and kept there for a moment or two before being removed. Not only does it hurt, but they cannot understand why two such kind people – their mother and the doctor – should suddenly want to cause them pain. They cannot understand at that stage what an injection is or that it is for their own good.

Sometimes this sort of fear can be the result of apprehension on the part of an adult. The child who sees his or her mother grimace when she tells her husband she has made an appointment with her dentist will realize that there is something unnerving about dentists, even if no word has been spoken. And, of course, if no-one takes *them* to the dentist until they are in pain or need drastic treatment, they cannot be expected to become accustomed to the dental surgery and to the people who work there.

If the child has been taken to visit a relative in hospital – and particularly if there has been a death of someone while in hospital – they may well have come to associate hospitals and doctors with death in every case. As adults we all tend to forget that children are not born with the knowledge and understanding we have acquired through experience and that many things need to be put into actual words to dispel those inner fears.

Fear of pain is, of course, self-perpetuating. Anyone, adult or child, who is frightened will automatically tense their muscles. And, because a tensed body feels even greater pain, the experience will be just as bad as they dreaded and their fears will be reinforced, making things even more difficult on the next occasion. Any child who is old enough to understand can be taught basic relaxation, and once they are relaxed the amount of pain experienced will be significantly reduced. The knowledge that they have considerable control over the amount of pain they feel will allow their self-confidence to grow and their faith in the medical profession in general to return.

Phobias

A phobia is an illogical fear. The person does not exist who is not nervous about something, whether it is being stung by a wasp or bitten by a dog. Such general anxieties, provided they are kept in proportion, are merely a form of self-preservation.

Children's phobias are often the result of adult fears. A very young child automatically assumes that adults are wise and power-ful beings and, should such a wonderful person demonstrate – albeit unknowingly – that he or she is frightened of something, that fear will often appear in a vastly magnified form in the child.

Mandy's mother had been bitten by a dog when she was herself a child. Throughout her childhood she had remained nervous of dogs in general and big dogs in particular but, as she grew up, she managed to conquer this fear – although she never voluntarily touched a dog and would certainly not have wanted to keep one as a pet. When Mandy was born her mother was determined to hide her fears, as she did not want her little girl growing up to be afraid of dogs. No longer did she cross the road to avoid an oncoming dog. She did not even allow herself to react when, while visiting the home of a friend, the family dog came and sat by her feet. Or that is what she thought. Perhaps there was something in her expression or perhaps she merely tightened her grip on Mandy's hand when a dog approached but, for whatever reason, the child was obviously able to sense her mother's fear and soon started to demonstrate the same anxieties herself.

At the risk of sounding sexist, it is a fact that young girls will often encourage each other to scream or run away when confronted by spiders or other insects. As time goes by the original cause of these fears may well be forgotten while the fear itself remains.

Many adults actually make the situation far worse by trying to dispel the phobia either by mocking the child or by forcing them to confront the object of which they are terrified without any previous preparation. There is no point in compelling a child who is petrified of water (for whatever reason) to jump into the swimming pool. Nor can the child who has a horror of spiders be helped by having a large hairy one placed on their hand. But what about those adults who, no doubt out of kindness, pander to their child's phobia? 'Little Johnny is so frightened of birds that we always cross the road if we see a group of sparrows pecking at some crumbs on the pavement ahead,' or 'We never go abroad for a holiday; Mary is really scared of flying.'

The only way in which to help a child (or adult for that matter) to overcome a phobia is to talk gently to them about it, and to explain the situation logically. Then perhaps you can show them pictures of whatever it is that they fear; if they are old enough, they can look the subject up in a book or encyclopaedia so that they really know all about it. The idea is not to make them love something that previously terrified them but to put the whole matter in proportion, so that they no longer have an illogical fear that could possibly affect the whole of the rest of their life.

Lying

There is no real need to pay too much attention to the far-fetched tales of a child under the age of six or seven; these could merely be the telling of fanciful stories rather than deliberate untruths. In a child over seven, however, the telling of lies is a deliberate act and should be recognized as such. Of course lying to get out of trouble or to escape punishment – 'It wasn't me' – is quite understandable. That does not mean, however, that it should not be discouraged. Other forms of lying tend to be symptomatic of deep-rooted problems within the child themselves, often indicating that they feel unloved and inadequate, or insecure and lacking in confidence. The only way in which they can feel more important, whether it is to their family or their peers, is to tell lies about their possessions, ability or background. In many cases they will know that they are bound to be caught out in the end, but they will persist in telling the lies none the less. If you find when you receive his or end-of-term report that your child has been lying to you about their school grades, perhaps you should ask yourself why they have felt compelled to do this, knowing that you would discover the truth as soon as the report reached you. Are you perhaps expecting too much of them? Do you show anger or disappointment when their marks are lower than you think they should be? Perhaps they feel that the only way to gain love is by being clever – and perhaps they need that love so much that it is even worth anger or punishment when the truth finally comes to light.

Other children tell seemingly pointless lies. It was only after listening to the chatter of a group of children in the school playground that Peter's mother discovered that her son had been lying to her. While in the car on the way home she and Peter would always talk about what had happened in school that day and on most days she would ask him what he had eaten for lunch. The child would answer quite readily but what his mother found later was that he never gave her a truthful answer. There seemed to be no reason at all for this. Peter was quite a good eater and had no marked food dislikes and it really did not seem to be important whether the school canteen had served up mince or spam that day. So why was her son lying to her about such a trivial matter?

When a child lies for no apparent reason – it doesn't get them out of a tight corner, nor does it make them appear more important – the actual subject matter about which they have lied is rarely significant. What is important is that such telling of untruths is generally symptomatic of stress or anxiety in that child, and it is this which needs investigating.

Stealing

The child who takes what does not belong to them often has no need of the items they steal. What they often do need in such circumstances is more positive proof that they are loved and wanted. It is frequently the child of undemonstrative parents who steals. This does not mean, of course, that his or her parents do not love them; merely that the parents may find it more difficult to express that love to the child. (We are not discussing here the child from the difficult or under-privileged background where the lack of love may be more obviously recognized – that is a separate matter.)

If you discover that your child has been stealing from you or others – and it is of paramount importance that you do not accuse them of this unless you are absolutely certain of your facts – all the shouting and punishment in the world will not solve the problem; they will merely become more clever at it as they grow older. They must know that you *know* what they have been doing and you can, if you wish, ask them why they have been stealing; but most young children will not be able to give you an answer. Although they must be told that it is wrong and that you do not want them to do it any more, they must also be reassured that you still love them and will continue to do so.

If a child steals things to give them to others, he or she is obviously trying to 'buy' their friendship. This means that, for whatever reason, he or she does not think that anyone would like them enough to want to be their friend without this 'bribery'. Why is this? Could they be jealous of a new baby in the family, or the achievements of an older brother or sister – perhaps one to whom they have been unfavourably compared?

About three months after the birth of her baby brother, nine-year-old Philippa began to steal money from her mother's purse. She then spent every penny she had taken on presents for her mother – flowers, bars of chocolate, magazines – and nothing at all on herself. Although she was intelligent enough to understand just why her mother had to spend so much time caring for the new baby, after nine years of being an only child Philippa was not able to cope with what appeared to her to be her mother's rejection of her. Fortunately, her mother soon discovered what was happening – after all, not many nine-year-old children have enough money to buy presents for their mother every week – and was able to make sure that she and her daughter spent time together when the baby was asleep and that Philippa was allowed to play her part in caring for 'her' baby.

Children hate to feel 'different' to their contemporaries. Adam's parents were determined that he would not be allowed to eat junk food, but only food that was good for him. Consequently sweets, chocolate, crisps and the like were outlawed from the outset. All went well until Adam went to school, where he discovered that all his friends were eating things he wasn't allowed to. He begged his mother to let him eat them too – a request which was summarily turned down. From that time on Adam began to steal. Sometimes he took the other children's sweets from their pockets; sometimes he stole money to buy them for himself. He didn't even care for the taste of all these forbidden items; it was just that he could not cope with the feeling of deprivation and of being different. So perhaps the answer is to allow such things in moderation when they will cease to have any real importance.

Changes in drawings and paintings

Naturally, children's drawings and paintings change all the time as they grow and develop, so what we are dealing with here is not one isolated example but a trend. Look at several of your child's drawings – say eight to ten of them taken over a period of two or three weeks. Remember to make allowances for lack of ability but then study the pictures, particularly if you can see noticeable differences. Even when the child is not suffering from any form of stress, this interesting exercise will give definite clues to their character.

Dramatic changes over a short period of time will often indicate an inner sense of anxiety.

- Those who draw only on the left-hand half of the page tend to be more introverted than those who draw on the right. If the drawing covers the whole page it is usually an indication that the child is quite sociable, and able to mix and communicate with both their peers and their elders.
- If just the top half of the page is used, the child is probably a day-dreamer. The more practical child and the one who likes physical action are more likely to use the bottom of the paper.
- Remembering that younger children tend to press heavily with a pencil, you will generally find that the lighter the pressure the more sensitive the child. Very heavy pressure, particularly in an older child, may indicate feelings of anxiety.
- Very angular drawings may be signs of aggression or hostility, whereas more rounded ones are usually done by the emotional and openly loving child.
- Most young children choose to paint in primary colours. Too much black paint (apart, perhaps, from outlines) is often a sign of insecurity.

17

- Ask your child to draw a picture of a house and then study it, bearing in mind all the above points. Now look at the house itself. If you can see lots of detail – windows, curtains, flowers in the garden, etc. – the child probably feels secure in his or her home life.

When Martin was asked to draw a picture of a house all he put on paper was a simple outline and the front door plus two dots to indicate windows. He also placed the house very much on the left-hand half of the paper. When all these points were considered it became obvious that Martin felt insecure at home and was unable to show warmth and affection to others.

Warning signs

These are important only when they appear regularly; ignore an isolated instance.

- great distortion;
- very heavy pressure;
- omission of detail: doors and windows on houses, limbs and eyes on people;
- if the picture is of a family group, note the relative sizes of the figures and see whether any one person is constantly left out;
- arms always raised above the level of the head;
- if more than half the picture is in red (unless this is called for, as in drawings of fire engines, etc.), this is a sign of suppressed aggression;
- too much black may be an indication that the child is not happy. The occasional black picture (night sky with stars for example) is not to be considered a problem. However, should a great many of the paintings be predominantly black, there is usually some underlying insecurity.

Checklist 1

Study the statements on the page opposite and put a tick against the ones that apply to your child. The more ticks you make, the more likely it is that the child is suffering from some sort of stress, whether temporary or permanent, and is in need of your help. (Only tick

Checklist 1	
My child:	Yes
is aggressive	
cries often	
has temper tantrums	
sleeps badly	
has nightmares	
wakes frequently	
wets the bed	
is often irritable	
is frightened of anything new	
dislikes change	
eats very little	
is faddy about food	
eats too much	
complains of tummy aches	
is often frightened	
fears doctors, dentists, hospitals	
is very timid	
is very shy	

is a bully
shows disruptive behaviour
lies often
steals
shows a dramatic change in drawings/paintings

those statements which apply frequently, not just on the odd occasion.)

If the answer to any of these statements is 'yes', try and keep a note of when the symptom shows itself and, if possible, whether any significant incident appeared to trigger it off.

Checklist 2

Any of the events listed in Checklist 2 could be responsible for causing anxiety in your child. Study the list and see whether one or more have happened recently.

You could also see whether your child reacts differently on school or other days; whether any particular person seems to cause anxiety in him or her or whether there is any specific house they do not like to visit.

Having done what you can to recognize the symptoms and to pinpoint the cause of the problem, you have to decide how to deal with the situation; and hopefully you will find many of the answers in Part Two.

Checklist 2

birth of new baby

death of relative, friend (or even pet)

separation, divorce

frequent family arguments

move of home

change of school

one parent temporarily away from home

hospital stay

new teacher

new school subject

PART TWO
How Stress In Children Is Caused

2
Coping with Divorce or Separation

It is a sad fact that, at the time of writing, one marriage in every three ends in divorce. Each year 150,000 children under the age of 16 are involved in what is an enormous emotional trauma. If you add to that number all those children whose parents' relationship is in the process of breaking down, even if divorce has not yet been mentioned, you will see just how vast a problem this is.

With each year that passes an ever-increasing number of parents find that they are having to try and explain the situation to their children at a time when they themselves are going through a tremendous emotional upheaval. And yet the way in which they make these explanations and the reassurance and comfort they are able to give their sons and daughters at this time are vitally important when viewed in the context of the future emotional life of those children.

It is not only the child's immediate future that is at risk, although much loving help will be needed if he or she is to cope successfully with this traumatic disruption in their home life. We also have to remember that the children of today are the husbands and wives of tomorrow, and that the way in which they deal with their own future emotional relationships may be greatly influenced by the way they are helped to cope with the present situation.

This is not the place to discuss whether it is better for children to deal with the separation of their parents or to have to live in a household where it is obvious that the love those parents formerly had for each other has gone and where arguments and bitterness fill each day. The decision as to whether or not they should part is the responsibility of each individual couple. Although the number of divorces and separations provides a sad statistic, it cannot be thought that it would be better to turn back the clock and force unhappy couples to stay together. So, realizing that divorce is here to stay and that the children will always be the innocent victims, we have to start from that point and consider what can be done to help them through what is bound to be a very difficult time indeed.

However difficult it may be, it is vitally important that you do not allow your children to become involved in the adults' arguments. It is far better if you can keep the problems between the two of you separate from whatever family life still remains. But this does not mean that you should have violent rows behind closed doors and then sit down at the supper table stony-faced and either not talking to each other at all or passing bitter and sarcastic remarks. Whatever the adult problems, they are not the fault of the children and so their lives must be made as trouble-free as possible. After all, if a separation proves to be inevitable, they are going to have a great deal to cope with soon enough.

Of course, children are by no means stupid. However much you try to hide the situation from them, they will soon become aware that something is wrong – even if they do not know what it is. Because their imaginations are so vivid, they may even assume that what is happening is something even more dreadful than it really is, so it is obvious that the sooner you are able to sit down and talk to them the better it will be. Once you realize that a separation is inevitable, you owe it to your children to put them in the picture.

Ideally these discussions should be planned between you and your partner and you should sit down together to talk to your children. In some cases this is naturally not possible; perhaps one partner has already left the family home or perhaps the atmosphere between the two of you is so bad that you are not even able to speak to each other about a topic as important as your children's welfare. If that is the case, then it is better for you to talk to them alone than to leave them to wait and wonder.

The essential starting point for any such conversation is to reassure your children that, even if mummy and daddy do not love each other any more, there has been no change in the love they feel towards *them*. Even if your partner has gone and has now set up home with someone else – and however difficult you may find it to say – you must tell your child that you know their father loves them and that you hope that they will see him soon. Such conversations between warring parents and their children are obviously difficult, but if your children are to be spared even more stress and anxiety than they are already going to have to face, then you have to put them first.

It is also important that you reassure your child that they are in no way to blame for the break-up of the marriage. Adults often do not realize that many children assume that, had they been 'better' or 'different', their parents would have stayed together.

After ten years of marriage, Paula and Anthony realized that they no longer wished to live together, even though neither of them had found anyone else. The divorce was as amicable as it is possible to be and, before Anthony left the family home, both parents sat down with their two sons, aged eight and four, and explained the situation as best they could. They told them that both mummy and daddy loved them very much and that, although daddy was going to live in another house, they would be able to see him as often as they wished. The children seemed to accept the situation but, some months after the actual divorce, eight-year-old Jeremy became very distressed and suffered from many of the more obvious anxiety symptoms. When Paula tried to talk to him and find out what was the matter, Jeremy sat on his mother's lap and sobbed. Eventually he asked her: 'If I do better at school, will daddy come back and live with us again?' It was only then that she realized that young Jeremy had become convinced that his father had gone away because he was so disappointed in his son's scholastic prowess. (In fact, Jeremy's school work had only deteriorated after he had become subconsciously aware of the pre-separation friction in the family home.) Fortunately in this case Paula and Anthony were on good enough terms to present a united front and to reassure their little boy that the divorce had nothing whatsoever to do with his school work and that he was in no way to blame for the break-up of the marriage.

In this case, Jeremy's symptoms of distress had been so obvious that Paula could not have failed to observe them. Also the young boy was quite open and articulate and was able to tell his mother what the problem was. But of course this is not so in every case. That is why it is up to you to keep an eye on your child, to see whether they are exhibiting any of the signs of stress or anxiety indicated in Part One. Only then will you be able to deal with the situation.

It is understandably difficult for any parent who feels that they have been 'wronged' not to pass on such feelings to their child. But, even if your partner has left you for someone else, it is vitally important that you try not to refer to him or her as 'bad', 'cruel' or 'wicked'. It is naturally very tempting, if you are the parent with custody (and this is usually the woman) to take every opportunity to criticize your ex-partner and to belittle him in the eyes of the child. It is even more tempting to be scathing about his new partner, if he has one, but your child may well be meeting that new partner in the near future and the meeting will be less traumatic for them if you have not been too vitriolic about her.

As soon as you possibly can, try and explain to the child what will be the practical arrangements for the future. Children hate any form of insecurity and will want to know what lies ahead. Who will they live with – and why? Will they be able to stay in the same house and go to the same school, or will they have to move? How often and under what circumstances will they be able to see the parent who is leaving? What will happen in the school holidays? If you are not sure of the answers to these or any other questions they might have, tell them so and reassure them that, as soon as details have been worked out, you will put them in the picture. Try, if you can, to keep as much as possible of their everyday life the same as it has been. All children, and particularly the younger ones, will find it easier to cope if there is as little change in their day-to-day life as possible. If the home and school surroundings remain the same, they will find it easier to cope with the inevitable emotional upheaval.

Children of different ages react very differently to the trauma of parental separation. Although, naturally, there are exceptions to every rule, what follows is an indication of the anxieties usually suffered by each age group.

Small children

Children under the age of four or five are not always able to understand the situation or to voice their fears. In many cases their greatest concern may be that, one parent having left them, the other will soon abandon them too. They may become clinging and possessive or revert to previously outgrown baby habits, such as bedwetting, thumb-sucking, baby talk, etc.

A child of this age will often express the desire to share your bed at night after the departure of the other parent. Tempting as it may be to allow this – after all, it will bring you a certain amount of comfort, as well as them – you will be making a rod for your own back and laying the foundation for future problems. It is far better for you to sit in their room until they fall asleep at night, having explained to them, if they are old enough to understand, that you will then be sleeping in your own bed.

Five to eight

Children of this age will often demonstrate an outward acceptance of the whole situation and then, some time after the event, go on to exhibit many of the symptoms detailed in Part One. You should keep a particular watch on the behaviour of a child in this age group – although try not to let them see that you are doing so.

Dr Judith Wallerstein runs the Center for the Family in Transition in California. Because five- to eight-year-olds find it difficult to put their deep emotional feelings in words, she encourages them to express their anxieties by drawing pictures or playing with dolls and often finds their behaviour very indicative of the emotional upheaval they are experiencing.

One child put the mummy doll in one corner of the room and the daddy doll in the opposite one. Another made them have fights, banging them together violently (although the parents in this case had not actually been physically violent towards one another). Yet another drew picture after picture of himself, his sister and his dog – neither parent being portrayed at all.

Dr Wallerstein emphasizes that children of this age are most likely to experience guilt and feel that they have been the cause of the break-up of their parents' marriage. Somewhat more optimistically she also feels that, with assistance – whether from a professional or from caring parents – they can outgrow that feeling and be helped to survive without any permanent emotional damage.

It is the child of this age, too, who is most likely to try playing off one parent against the other. It is a form of emotional bullying, only emphasizing to the observant adult the inner insecurity the child is experiencing. This does not mean, however, that you should ever give in to this sort of blackmail; merely that its very existence should make you aware that your child is, in their own way, crying out for help.

Samantha's parents divorced when she was seven. Father went off to live with his new partner, who later became his second wife, while mother stayed in the family home with Samantha and her older sister Fiona. Fiona, at fourteen, refused to have anything at all to do with her father and his new wife and became fiercely loyal to her mother. Samantha, however, appeared to accept the situation quite well. She lived with her mother and sister during the week and spent weekends with her father, whose new home was only a few miles away.

After a month or two Samantha returned from each weekend visit clutching progressively more expensive gifts from her father – things that her mother was in no financial position to afford, even had she considered them appropriate. It was only after the child had boasted to her older sister that she could 'get anything out of Daddy' that the situation was investigated. It appeared that Samantha had persuaded her father to buy her anything she wanted by threatening that, if he didn't, she wouldn't come and see him any more. Already distressed by his elder daughter's behaviour and feeling a certain amount of guilt about breaking up the family, James had been afraid that he would lose contact with his younger child too and had given in to her emotional blackmail to prevent this from happening.

Sensing that her mother was feeling unhappy and vulnerable about what she saw as her ex-husband's betrayal, but knowing that she did not have sufficient money for expensive presents, Samantha had used the same sort of blackmailing tactics to get treats and privileges for herself at home. If her mother would not allow her to stay up to watch a particular television programme or if she tried to persuade her to do her school homework, Samantha would threaten that she would go and live permanently with Daddy. Having been deserted by one member of her family, her mother was anxious that she should not be deserted by another and so she often gave in to Samantha's demands.

All this might make it sound as if Samantha was a horrible little girl, but in reality she was just a very unhappy one. She was extremely distressed by the break-up of the family and her blackmailing behaviour was really a desperate cry for help. She had no intention of leaving her mother and sister, and she didn't even want the items she persuaded her father to buy for her. But to her these gifts and treats symbolized love; she was so unconvinced that her parents loved her that she needed the constant reassurance of material objects or personal privileges to prove it.

Ten to twelve

The child of this age will frequently be openly angry with his or her parents, with the situation and with the world at large. This in turn can lead to behavioural problems at home and at school. They may appear rude and rebellious towards their parents and teachers, and may experience difficulties in their relationships with friends of their own age.

Problems at school can take many forms. Work may well suffer and they may be insolent or even begin to play truant. It is always advisable to inform your child's form teacher quietly of the situation when there is a divorce, separation or other significant disruption in family life, but particularly with children of this age. In this way, although the teacher cannot permit them to get away with disruptive behaviour in class, allowances will be made until they have been helped to overcome their own anxieties.

This is the age, too, where the child is most likely to feel responsible for the parent with whom they live – and this is most often the mother. This situation applies whether the child is a son or a daughter; the son feels that he is now the 'man of the family' while the daughter feels that she is able to identify with her mother.

Helena was almost twelve when her father left, not only the family home, but also the country, to live in Australia. Although he had promised to pay maintenance to his ex-wife and their only child, this soon stopped and, despite a court order, the fact that he was so far out of the court's jurisdiction made the order unenforceable. Diane, Helena's mother, worked full time, so although they were certainly not wealthy, they managed to exist reasonably comfortably – although there was very little left over for luxuries.

Helena would arrive home from school each day about an hour before her mother returned from work. Without being asked, she immediately assumed responsibility for preparing their evening meal and, by the time Diane arrived, the table would be laid and the vegetables prepared. Diane really appreciated her daughter's assistance, and told her so. But gradually Helena started to take on responsibility for more and more of the household tasks so that, almost before Diane knew it, her daughter was doing more in the house than she was. When she tried gently to tell Helena that, grateful as she was for her help, perhaps it would be better for them to share the housework between them so that she could have more time to spend on her homework or just being with her friends, Helena insisted that she did not want to go out with the other girls but would prefer to stay at home with her mother.

All at once Diane realized that it had been several months since Helena had visited one of her schoolfriends or invited one of them home. Guiltily she realized that she had quite enjoyed the situation that had crept up on her. It was very pleasant to have someone to help with the household chores, and even more agreeable to have company in the evenings and at weekends. It helped to compensate for the loneliness and sense of being abandoned that she had felt immediately after the divorce and her ex-husband's failure to provide financially even for his daughter. But she had allowed herself to forget that Helena was still a child and that she needed the company of friends of her own age. So, one evening, she sat down with her daughter and discussed the whole situation with her. Choosing her words carefully because she did not want Helena to think that she did not enjoy her help and her company, she explained that she was now perfectly content to be on her own whenever the girl wanted to spend time with her schoolfriends.

Over twelve

Those who come into this age group are often hardest hit by a family divorce or separation. They are no longer children but they are not yet adult and so, even when all is well at home, this is a time of physical and emotional turmoil for them. They are better able to cope with the problems in their own lives when home is the stable place it should ideally be. When they do not have that stability behind them they can experience a far more difficult adolescence.

Young people of this age are confronted with decisions of all sorts and a great deal of pressure is put on them by their peers who might be trying to persuade them to experiment with sex, alcohol, drugs, etc. If they feel that they are unable to turn to their families – even though they might never admit that they would want to – this is a time when the wrong decisions could well be made.

Anxiety in a boy or girl of this age may show itself in the form of aggressive speech or behaviour, rebelliousness, promiscuity or addiction. So, however difficult it might be, it is vital to convince them that the home is still a place of stability, even though there might now only be one parent living there.

It does not necessarily follow that children from broken homes are bound to repeat the pattern in their own adult lives. In fact, having been so close to the situation, many of them are even more determined not to make the same mistakes as their parents. And, while it is sad that there are now so many divorces, at least they do not feel too 'different' – something any child hates – because so many of their companions are experiencing a similar situation.

The checklists below indicate several ways in which you can help your child survive the break-up of his or her parents' relationship with the minimum amount of stress or anxiety. Naturally it is not possible to avoid stress altogether when the child's whole world seems to him to be falling apart. But with a little forethought and careful planning you can certainly reduce the long-term ill effects of that stress.

When the relationship is in the process of breaking down

- Never involve the child in any arguments or disputes between you and your partner. Try and keep that side of your life separate and do your best – even though it may be difficult – to present a reasonably calm front to your child.
- Because your child will be well aware that there is something wrong – even if they cannot identify that 'something' – it is vitally important that both their father and mother keep reassuring them that they love him or her. This will prevent the child feeling that they are in some way responsible for the change in their parents' relationship.
- Whatever your feelings about your partner – and even if you feel that you are the one who has been wronged – do your best not to criticize the other parent too much in front of the child. This

would cause them to have divided loyalties and could be extremely stress-inducing.

- Whatever stage your own relationship may have reached, never use your child as a 'go-between'. This is a sad reflection on parents who may be living in the same house, but who find that they are unable to communicate with each other on even the most mundane level. Asking your child to 'Tell your father that dinner is on the table', because you yourself feel unable to say this, is putting them in an intolerable position.

Once you have decided to separate or divorce

- Tell your child as soon as you can find an opportune moment. However young they may be, they will be fully aware – even if it is subconscious – that things are going wrong and, if you don't explain to them what the situation is, they may well imagine something even worse.
- If at all possible, you and your partner should explain the situation to your child together. Face them with the facts, explaining them gently but not leaving room to hope that you will change your minds. Try to keep the conversation as free as you can from bitterness and acrimony.
- If you find that, for whatever reason, you have to explain the situation to your child on your own, do not – for your child's sake – use the occasion as an opportunity for criticizing the other parent in his or her absence.
- Remember to emphasize that, although Mummy and Daddy do not love each other any more, they *both* love their child as much as ever and that the breakdown of the marriage is in no way his or her fault.
- However young your child may be, tell them the truth. It may be easier at the time to say that 'Daddy has gone away for a while', but you will be storing up innumerable future problems for yourself. Not only will you have to tell them the truth one day, but they may hear it from someone else first. In either case they will never again feel that they are able to trust you or to rely on your word – so how can they believe you when you say you love them or that they are not to blame?
- At all stages try to avoid putting the blame for the break-up on

34

the other parent. It is very rare for this to be the truth in any case but, even if it is and even if it makes you feel better for a moment or two to tell your son or daughter just what their father or mother has done, that moment or two of selfish satisfaction could cause years of unhappiness for your child.

- Your child will need reassurance at this time that they will still be able to see the departing parent. If, as is sometimes the case, their father (for it is more often the man) is moving so far away that regular meetings are difficult to arrange, let your child know that they can still keep in touch by means of letters and telephone calls and perhaps that they will be able to visit their father in the holidays. All this will help to confirm that the departing parent still loves them and is not abandoning them.

- Most children worry about the practicalities of their future. As soon as you can, explain what is going to happen about living accommodation, schooling and so on. It will help your child if as few changes can be made in home and school life as possible, as they need to feel that something is going to be constant and stable at what is obviously a highly traumatic time.

After the separation

- Children of all ages – even the older ones – need constant reassurance that they are loved by both parents and that they were in no way to blame for their separation.

- It will be necessary, especially in the early stages, to be tolerant and understanding of changes in your child's behaviour. They will simply be reacting to the trauma of their parents' separation. But being understanding does not mean allowing them to get away with behaviour that you find intolerable, or becoming overindulgent and showering them with presents in an attempt to 'buy' their happiness. Indeed, if you have always been reasonably firm, it will make them even more disorientated should you suddenly change your attitude now.

- Make sure that all access arrangements are honoured where possible. It is not difficult for the custodial parent to turn the child's mind against the one who has left, but please, for your child's sake, never be tempted to do this. If you have a young child and they have to be taken to visit his father, never say such

35

things as 'I'm not going near that man's house.' Access visits, with their often tearful greetings and partings, are difficult enough for any child without you removing the stabilizing influence of your presence immediately before and after they have taken place. And, knowing that you are doing it for your child's sake, will it really hurt you to be civil to your ex-partner for the few moments it takes to deliver your child into his or her care?

- The child who is able to talk to you about their feelings immediately after their parents' separation is less likely to suffer stressful after-effects. Allow them to tell you what they are feeling and try to help them deal with what is happening in their world. Apart from helping them over the immediate situation, you will also be setting a healthy precedent for the future. The teenager who is able to talk to his or her parents is considerably less likely to go off the rails.

- If, as is often the case, your financial situation is worse after the separation, try and explain this to the older child – not to apportion blame for the reduction in available money, but so that they understand why some of the luxuries they previously took for granted are no longer available. Even quite young children are able to understand simple explanations about money, and in this way they will not think that fewer treats mean that they are being punished for their part in the break-up of the partnership.

- Let your child become involved in what you do. Talk to them about what is going on at the present and about plans for the future. Allow them to play their part in helping you around the house – remembering always not to let them feel that they have to be with you at all times at the expense of their own social life.

- As soon as possible find the time to have a quiet word with your child's form teacher so that he or she knows what is going on. In this way they can keep an eye on your son or daughter, and can be a little more tolerant of any episodes of tearfulness or lapses in behaviour.

Helping the child of another divorced person

- Find the time to listen sympathetically to them; perhaps they find it easier to talk to you than to either of their own parents.

- Never try to pretend that his or her parents' separation has not happened or that you know nothing about it. It is far better to refer to it gently and sympathetically.
- If he or she is a visitor in your house, try not to single them out for preferential treatment just because you feel sorry for them. This over-compensation will not be helpful as it will merely succeed in making them feel 'different' – something all children hate.
- Whatever your own views – and even if one parent happens to be a close personal friend – never criticize either their father or mother to the child, as it will cause considerable anxiety in his or her own mind as to the truth of the situation and the culpability of either or both parents.

3

The Child Victim

We all tend to think – or perhaps prefer to think – that it is only strangers who abuse children. But, in fact, in more than 75% of reported cases of sexual abuse the abuser is someone known to the child. It can be a 'friend', a relative or even a parent and often the abuse continues over a long period of time with the child being too frightened to say anything about it. Where forms of abuse other than sexual are concerned, a previous relationship with the abuser is even more likely. Indeed, in many cases of physical violence against a child the abuser is either a parent or someone in a similar position.

Abuse of any sort not only does physical harm to the child, but also has a truly devastating emotional and psychological effect upon them, as then their instinctive trust in those closest to them is betrayed. This feeling of betrayal is even greater when, even if only one person is involved in the actual abuse, the other stands by and does nothing to help – or, even worse, covers up the situation so that no outsider knows what is happening. In my work as a hypnotherapist I see many adults who were abused as children and I know just how much their entire life has been affected by what took place many years ago.

The number of children who suffer abuse is far greater than most people would suppose, and this by no means merely applies to today's society. The adults who consult me for help now were children 20, 30, 40 or even 50 years ago and they are still trying to come to terms with the disastrous effects of their childhood. The only difference now is that, fortunately, things have been brought far more out into the open and children are being encouraged to talk about what has been happening to them.

There are three basic types of child abuse.

1. *Physical violence*, where the intention is to inflict pain on the child.
2. *Mental and emotional abuse*, which is just as real and just as harmful but leaves no outwardly visible scars that other people might recognize.

3. *Sexual abuse*, which is for the gratification of the abuser rather than the punishment of the child.

One emotion is common to every child who has ever been abused, and that is guilt. It may be hard for the outsider to understand just why the child should accept the blame for violence shown towards them, but it is a reaction common to every case. A child looks upon their mother and father (or those in that position) as important, wise and all-powerful people who can do no wrong. If, however, one of them should turn round and do him or her harm, the young child's subconscious mind reasons that for this wonderful being to inflict harm or demonstrate anger towards him, they (the children) must be very bad indeed and deserving of such treatment. Even when, as they grow older, their logic tells them that this was not, in fact, true, none the less that subconscious programming is so great it is quite capable of overriding all logical thought. Those adults who now come to consult me are still being affected by that early effect upon their subconscious minds, even when their own common sense allows them to see the truth of the situation.

Physical violence

I am not concerned here with a parent smacking a naughty child for a minor misdemeanour. Whether or not one thinks that such chastisement achieves anything apart from an immediate release of pent-up anger or frustration for the adult is not for discussion here. Nor am I talking about bullying by someone of the child's own age – that will be dealt with in Chapter 5. What I am dealing with here are constant or prolonged episodes of physical violence, usually in the home, some of which are severe enough to result in the physical disfigurement or even the death of the child victim – and all of which are certainly responsible for severe emotional scarring.

Such acts of violence are setting a pattern for the child's future life. It is no coincidence that statistics show that a child who has been the victim of physical violence often grows up to become either a perpetrator of such violence or else a perpetual victim.

Let me tell you about Sandra, one of my patients. When Sandra was a child her father was frequently drunk and would return home from the pub to inflict physical violence upon Sandra, her mother and her younger sister. The subconscious mind of that terrified little girl accepted the image of herself as a victim, deserving only of such treatment, and sadly this is how Sandra continued to see herself as she grew up. At 17, desperate to escape from home, she became pregnant by a 30-year-old man whom she later married. This man, unsurprisingly, turned out to be just as violent towards Sandra as her father had been. I say 'unsurprisingly' because what Sandra had done was unconsciously to choose a man who would continue to treat her as she inwardly felt she should be treated. It was only when her husband began to be violent towards their young son that Sandra found the courage to leave him and make a fresh start. By the time I saw her – when she was 32 – she had been involved in two more relationships with men who were violent towards her. At that point she suddenly came to her senses and realized that she needed help if she were ever to be able to stop seeing herself as a potential victim. She finally succeeded, but it was a slow and difficult process involving the re-learning of basic emotions and beliefs.

Tim, on the other hand, had been brought up in a household consisting of a weak mother and a father who considered that it was a sign of being a 'real man' to drink, swear and womanize. This man was determined to show that he was master in his own home, and he would become violent towards his wife if his meal was late or if something in the house were not to his liking. He would shout abuse at Tim's little sister, but she soon became adept at sensing danger and would keep well out of her father's way. However, he never laid a finger on Tim, believing perhaps that violence should be shown only towards the women of the family.

As Tim grew older his father tried to mould him into his own concept of what a 'man' should be, encouraging his son to drink and to be physical in every way, even to indulging in sexual activities at a comparatively early age. It was partly fear of being thought a 'sissy' and partly a sort of admiration for what he saw as his father's 'manliness' that made Tim conform to the older man's ideas. Once he was adult he continued the pattern already set up: a pattern of drinking combined with verbal abuse and violence towards women. This, after all, fitted in with his subconscious image of what a man should be.

It is possible, in time and with professional help, for someone like

Tim to change his inner feelings and therefore his behaviour. For this to take place, however, the individual himself has to want to bring about such change. Sadly, Tim did not have the desire to alter his behaviour.

The basis for the adult lives of both Sandra and Tim was established in their early childhood. It is essential to protect your child as much as possible during their formative years so that they may go on to have as happy and fulfilled an adult life as circumstances permit.

So what can you do if you believe that a child is the subject or spectator of violent attacks by one of his or her parents?

If the child is yours

It is very rare for one parent to be violent towards their child and for the other parent not to know what is going on. If that second adult chooses to do nothing about the situation, then he or she is just as responsible for the psychological harm done to the child as is the one who is physically violent.

It is not always wise to try and confront a violent individual, and definitely not at the time when they are in a violent frame of mind. If there is no alternative, you must consider seeking outside help and doing what you can to escape from the situation, taking your child with you. Once you are free of immediate danger, you should seek professional help in dealing with the situation, to prevent it repeating itself.

If the child is not yours

The person who is most able to recognize signs of physical abuse in a child is often a teacher, a neighbour or some other caring adult who sees the child regularly. Perhaps you have noticed frequent scars, bruises or other signs of physical damage on the child. Perhaps you have heard screams from the family home, or perhaps you have just not seen them at all lately. Of course there could be natural explanations for all these things. Many children do go through a phase of being accident-prone; others have temper tantrums or nightmares and some may go to a friend or relative for a holiday. But if you have the slightest suspicion that all is not well, you should alert either the authorities or a child care agency who is equipped to investigate the matter further. Be wary of confronting the parents yourself as, if you are right in your fears, this could often incite the violent individual to further action against the unfortunate victim. It may even be that you will be thought of as a 'nosey-parker', but surely this is better than allowing violence against a young child to continue.

If you are in contact with the child him or herself, see if you can encourage them to talk to you. Of course, even if they wish to, they may feel some sort of misguided loyalty and refuse to speak out against one of their parents. If this is so, then once again the answer is to call in a professional who will be experienced in handling such matters.

Mental abuse

In some ways mental abuse can be just as frightening as physical violence and, as well as making the child's life a misery now, the long-term effects can be just as damaging to the future adult. I am naturally not referring to normal family discipline or scolding where this is appropriate, but to continuous accusations of stupidity or perpetual threatening of punishments that no-one ever intends to inflict. Ruling by fear is a form of cruelty in itself, and can influence a child's whole personality and psychological make-up.

In some cases a misguided adult may actually think that those belittling phrases they are constantly repeating will spur the child on to greater efforts, but the result is usually the complete opposite. Tell them often enough 'You're stupid!' 'You'll never learn,' 'Your sister could do it at your age,' or 'Why can't you be more like your brother?' and you will probably find that the child will give up trying altogether. After all, if they feel that they can never be successful, what is the point of making the attempt?

Some people are never satisfied. William is the son of parents who both enjoyed successful academic careers. Try as he might, William was never able to achieve great things at school, much to the regret of his somewhat authoritarian father. Although the child's one desire was to win his father's approval – and he worked extremely hard towards this end – he never quite succeeded. Instead of praising his son for his effort and for the standard he managed to reach, his father always seemed disappointed that the results had not been even better. When William, after putting in a lot of hard work and concentration, managed to obtain a grade B for a particular piece of work, his father's only comment was 'Why didn't you get an A?'

The constant wearing away of the child's self-esteem by these repeated expressions of disappointment or disapproval are bound to have a long-term effect. As one of my adult patients told me, 'I always knew I wasn't really stupid, but for seventeen years I was told that I was – so in the end I believed it.' This young woman had to leave home and go through a painful period of psychological readjustment before she was able to banish that belief from her subconscious mind.

There is a great deal of truth in the old adage that you should never make a threat or a promise that you do not intend to keep. Not only is it unkind and a betrayal of trust, but it can cause a great deal of emotional anxiety to a young child who tends to think that everything their parents say must be true. It is bad enough to promise a reward that is never forthcoming, but threats are even worse and can do real psychological harm.

If a child is to be punished for an episode of bad behaviour, that punishment should be meted out instantly – whether it means that they are sent to their room or told there and then that they will not watch television that evening – rather than issuing veiled threats. 'Wait until your father gets home' or even 'Just you wait' may seem quite innocuous phrases but they can result in constant feelings of apprehension for the child, or even a fear of their father due to the association in his mind of that man and some form of punishment. Even worse, of course, are threats of punishments that the adult knows perfectly well are never going to happen: 'You'll have to go and live in the children's home,' 'The police will take you away and lock you up.' One would think that parents today would be sufficiently enlightened not to use such phrases, but they are still heard and they still cause a great deal of stress to the young child to whom they are addressed.

The difference between this mental damage and the more commonly understood meaning of abuse – physical violence and sexual abuse – is that quite often the parent who inflicts such mental harm actually loves and cares for the child very much and would be shocked to think that they are actually hurting them in any way.

But, should your child be showing any of the symptoms of distress indicated below, perhaps you should ask yourself whether you, your partner or some other adult to whom the child looks up could inadvertently have been guilty of such treatment.

Signs of distress

- If he or she suddenly ceases to make any effort, whether in school or perhaps in some form of sport or hobby, there has to be a reason. Of course it is often possible that they have simply lost interest but often you will find that it is because someone has convinced them that, no matter how hard they may try, they will never succeed.
- If he or she begins to cheat to gain good marks, try asking yourself whether you have placed too great an emphasis on final results and too little on the amount of effort put in. Perhaps you are expecting them to excel in a subject that was your speciality, or to follow in your footsteps, without paying sufficient attention to their own aptitudes and interests.
- A child who seems to fear one of the adults with whom they are in regular contact will always have a reason for doing so. He or she may not tell you in so many words that they dread Daddy coming home because they have been told that their father will punish them for some earlier misdemeanour and they do not know what to expect, yet you only have to use a little imagination to realize how such a threat can escalate out of all proportion in the mind of a small child during the course of several hours.

What can you do?

- Talk to your child and find out why he or she has stopped trying or has begun to cheat. Always emphasize that you love them and are concerned about them and their problems, rather than accusing them of being lazy or dishonest.
- If you feel that you have been responsible for inflicting this stress upon your child – even if you never intended them to suffer in any way – ask yourself why you have done so. We would all like our children to do well, but why has it become so important that they excel? Are you perhaps living your life vicariously through them, so their success will in fact be yours?

- Try not to make any threats or promises that you do not intend to carry out – and carry them out as soon as possible.
- If you feel that it is your partner who is responsible for causing this anxiety in the child, find a time to talk the matter over between you and see if you can discover the cause.
- However much you love your child and want the best for them, remember that you could lose their trust and respect if you appear to be saying things you don't mean.
- Treat your child as an individual, with their own talents and shortcomings, rather than as someone who must grow up to be a carbon copy of you.

Sexual abuse

However much he or she may have been the innocent victim in a case of sexual abuse, a child will always feel guilty and responsible, both at the time and later throughout their life. Also, as many of my patients have sadly experienced, they will continue to feel 'unclean' and 'wicked', even though their logical mind may tell them that they did nothing wrong and what happened was forced upon them – often without any understanding of what was taking place.

All too often sexual abuse remains undetected – sometimes for years – as the child usually remains silent, whether because he or she has been threatened by their abuser or because they are afraid that no-one will believe them, or that they will be considered responsible. They may even successfully block out all memory of what has taken place, sometimes for years, only to suffer emotionally and psychologically in later life.

Carol came to me as a patient when she was 35. An attractive and intelligent woman, she could not understand why she had a terror of allowing any relationship to develop beyond a casual flirtation. Although she could not remember the occurrences consciously, when she was hypnotized she was able to recall being sexually abused by her father's brother when she was about eight. The young man had been acting as a baby-sitter. She had never told her parents as her uncle had convinced her that they would think she was so wicked that they would send her away. The abuse had continued over about a year, until her uncle moved to a different part of the country, after which Carol had succeeded in removing all recollection of it from her conscious memory. However, her subconscious mind had remembered only too well and had caused Carol to fear any close relationship with a man – sexual contact being linked in her mind with shame, pain and secrecy. Fortunately, after a course of hypnosis which allowed her to see the situation through 35-year-old eyes rather than the eyes of a terrified child, Carol was able to come to terms with what had happened all those years ago and to live a normal life.

Cases like that of Carol show how, even though the abuse itself may not last for years, the devastating effect upon the victim certainly does. Many people are unable to come to terms with what happened to them without professional assistance.

Unfortunately, many cases of sexual abuse occur between a parent and child in the child's own home. In one fell swoop the abuser is not only causing the child pain and suffering but also destroying his (or more often her) trust in adults and the feelings of security that home should be able to provide. It is also possible for one adult to be sexually abusing a child while the other adult in the home remains totally oblivious to what is going on – although it must be said that in many cases the second adult may have suspicions which he or she does not want to believe. Naturally no woman (for this is usually the case) wants to believe that the man she lives with would be capable of sexually interfering with her child, but such suspicions must always be investigated for the sake of the child's entire future.

It is vital that you encourage your child to talk to you about anything and everything and that you assure them that you believe what they tell you. This applies to many situations throughout childhood, but nowhere is it more important than in the area of sexual abuse. Distressing as it may be to discover what has been going on, it is far more distressing for the child if you disbelieve them, ignore the situation or cover up and lie to present a respectable front to the world at large.

If your child tells you that they have been sexually abused

- Encourage him or her to talk to you about it and show them that you believe what they have to tell you. Try not to appear shocked at whatever they might say, but persuade them to give you as many details as possible.

- Praise them for telling you. An abuser may well be put off continuing if he or she knows that the child and parent talk freely together.
- Reassure them of your love, and that they have not become unlovable in your eyes because of what has happened. Promise that you will do what you can to sort out the situation – and keep your promise.
- Explain that he or she is not guilty or wicked, and that what happened was not their fault.
- Do something about the situation, obtaining professional help where necessary. The abuser will need to be stopped and police should be informed, for the protection not only of your child but of others upon whom the abuser might force themselves. The child may well need counselling or professional assistance to deal with the situation so that they do not have to suffer decades (or even a lifetime) of psychological distress because of what has happened.

It has probably been extremely difficult for the child to tell you about what has happened in the first place. If he or she has trusted you sufficiently to do so, do not let them down by doing nothing about the situation – that way they will have been betrayed by two adults, not just one.

How to protect your child from sexual abuse

- Encourage him or her to talk to you about everything – good and bad – from when they are very little. Make time for them, listen to them and believe in them. A child who grows up knowing that they can discuss anything at all with their parents is far more likely to tell them should he or she be the victim of any form of abuse. The common abuser's threat that no-one will believe them will therefore be far less effective.
- Do not be embarrassed about discussing matters to do with sex or the human body with your child as soon as they wish to do so. Such discussions should naturally be kept at their level of understanding and interest; knowledge should not be forced upon them at too early an age, but remember that obvious discomfort on the part of an adult when talking about the body can lead to feelings of disgust or wickedness on the part of the child.

- If you find that there is one particular person with whom your child doesn't like to be left, or one particular house they don't like visiting, try and find out why. Do it gently, without making the child feel foolish or guilty. There may, of course, be a simple and innocent reason, but on the other hand, there may be some significance in these fears.

- If he or she does something wrong or naughty – however minor – and confesses to you, always praise them for owning up to it. That does not mean they should never be reprimanded, but if they are praised for their honesty they are far more likely to tell you about any possible abuse.

- Explain that his or her body is special and their own. Point out that, should they be confronted with any demonstrations of excessive affection from anyone that make them feel uncomfortable, then it is quite all right to say 'no'. Let them know that they should also tell you of any such approaches.

- Make sure an older child realizes that he or she can telephone you from anywhere at any time and you will come and get them if they wish without asking any questions at the time – although, of course, you would like later to be told why they needed you to come. Teach them to use a public telephone and ensure that they know not only their own telephone number but that of at least one friend or relative, and how to call 999.

- Explain that not all grown-ups are as kind and friendly as they might appear, although naturally you should try to do this in such a way that he or she does not immediately suspect all adults of harmful motives.

- If they are at school, see that they know who may collect them, whose car they may go in and whose houses they may visit. Tell them that, if they are ever unsure, they should contact you and ask.

- He or she must know that they should never go with someone they don't know, even if that person says that 'Mummy sent me'. One family I know even has a password that has to be used if someone else has to collect one or more of the children.

- Tell them that if they are at all worried they should ask a policeman or a traffic warden for help.

- Tell your child to scream, shout, run and make as much fuss as possible if someone tries to persuade them to get into a car or to come away with them, so that everyone notices. No would-be abductor is going to stay around to be the centre of attention.

- Convince them that they are right to refuse to go with anyone if they feel at all uncertain about them and that he or she will never be responsible for unwittingly offending a friend, as any genuinely well-meaning adult will not be in the least put out by their caution.

4

Dealing with Bereavement

The death of a person we love is a fact of life, and one with which we all have to deal at some time. It is often difficult enough for an adult to cope with the combination of practicalities and mixed emotions they are faced with when someone close to them dies; indeed, some do not really cope at all but continue to suffer for many years afterwards. But it is even more difficult for a young child to deal with that situation, and to do so satisfactorily needs the loving assistance of those adults closest to him or her, even though they themselves may well be in the throes of their own grief at the time.

Many of the emotional reactions of a child when he or she first encounters death will be similar to those experienced by the adult. But there will be others too. They are less likely to understand the concept of life and death, and may even associate dying with some sort of divine punishment for bad behaviour. The very words we use to bring comfort to them may only serve to add to their confusion. To say that someone has 'gone away' or 'gone to sleep' may well increase their anxieties about their own life. Will going on holiday or going to bed at night mean that they will die? He or she may find it difficult to understand what you mean when you tell them that someone they love has 'gone to Heaven' or 'gone to Jesus', as this means different things to different people; their reaction will depend very much on how great a part such religious terms have played in their life up to now.

Simon was only four when his grandmother died after a long period of ill health. His grandparents had lived several hundred miles from his own home and he had only seen them once or twice a year, so he was not really grief-stricken at the death, although he realized that something was wrong because he saw his mother crying when she received the news. Trying to explain to her young son what had happened, Simon's mother told him that 'Grandma has gone to be with Jesus' and the child accepted this without really understanding what was meant.

Although the family was a Christian one, none of them was a regular churchgoer. Indeed, the only times Simon had been to church were for his own christening and the wedding of a distant relative when he was just two years old – neither of which he could remember. So 'being with Jesus' did not convey a great deal to the child and he soon put the whole matter out of his mind.

A year later, when he was five and had just started school, Simon's parents felt that he should also attend Sunday School at the local church with the other children in the neighbourhood. They could not understand why their son began to suffer nightmares and to have tantrums every time this suggestion was put to him. They tried to emphasize that it would be fun: there would be games, singing and stories and he would be with lots of children of his own age. But in Simon's mind going to Sunday School had become synonymous with being with Jesus and, knowing that his grandmother had disappeared for ever, he felt that something terrible would befall *him* should his parents send him to this frightening place. It took a great deal of understanding and a lot of loving explanation before he was able to differentiate between his fears and reality.

If a child is old enough to understand what is going on, he or she should be allowed to take part in the grieving. Even a four-year-old can cope with the situation, although naturally things must be explained to them at their own level of comprehension. Talking about death, crying, asking questions – all these are essential if they are to learn to cope with bereavement, both now and in the future. It is not unusual for a well-meaning adult to send the child away 'until it's all over'. This is usually done for the child's own good, but it is actually the worst thing you can do. The child needs to be a part of the family loss and to work out his or her own sadness. Indeed, just having the child there can also be extremely beneficial to the grieving adult. Many people have said that they felt they would have coped far less well had they not had their children to care for at the time of their bereavement.

Gareth was only five years old when his father was killed in a road accident on his way home from work. His mother was naturally devastated when the sympathetic young policewoman came to break the news to her on that sunny afternoon. Wanting to shield her son from the anguish she was experiencing, she arranged to send him for a few days to a family friend who had a child of similar age – giving the friend instructions that the tragedy was not to be mentioned.

By the time Gareth returned home it was all over. The funeral had taken place and his mother, although still grief-stricken had regained her outward composure. Still wanting to protect her little boy, she told him that 'Daddy has gone to the angels' and that he would not be coming home any more. From that time onwards the matter was never talked about at all. If Gareth asked any questions about his father, he was always fobbed off with vague answers. His mother, thinking that it was for the best, never allowed her son to see her crying.

One night, hearing the sound of crying coming from Gareth's room, his mother went in to see what was wrong. She found her son in a very distressed state, convinced that he was responsible for his father leaving because he had sometimes been naughty. At that point, of course, his mother could see where her well-meaning actions had led and was able to comfort him, talk to him and explain the true situation in words that he could understand. For the first time mother and son sat and cried together. But suppose she had not heard him crying – imagine the permanent damage that could have been done to Gareth's emotional make-up, not to mention the feeling of betrayal he would experience when he was old enough to realize he had not been told the truth about so important a matter.

Just like every adult, each child should be allowed to go through the various stages of grief.

Unhappiness

Of course it is natural to feel unhappy when someone you love has been taken from you by death. The sense of loss can be so great it can seem like a physical pain that won't recede. It is also natural to be selfishly unhappy – the child will feel sorry for him or herself because they have no mother (or father or whoever it may be). They will be unhappy because this makes them 'different' – something any child (and many an adult) hates. He or she should not be scolded for such selfish thoughts – they are a normal part of the grieving process.

Fear

Whether the death has been sudden (as in an accident) or after a long illness, the very fact that someone can disappear from this world is enough to make the child frightened that the same thing could happen to them. If it is a parent who has died, then he or she may be terrified of losing the other one and being left all alone in the world. Most children who are old enough to think about death at all associate it with much older people and so the death of another child may cause a great deal of mental anguish as it immediately becomes a possibility that *they* too might die.

Loneliness

Although most adults can identify this feeling in themselves, most children will not realize that loneliness is what they are experiencing. It may show itself in many ways, the commonest being behaviour changes. Perhaps the child will become very clinging, as though holding on to whoever is still with them. Perhaps they will appear to be offhand, as if preparing themselves for yet another loss. Often they will simply become difficult to talk to or to reason with and, although they might never appear to want it, this is a time when physical closeness and comfort are of vital importance.

Anger

Many adults have been known to feel guilty because they feel so angry when they have been bereaved. Yet this too is a perfectly normal, and indeed essential, phase of grieving. Children always find their own anger difficult to cope with, and this is all the more pronounced when the anger follows the loss of someone they loved. They may be angry with the person who has died – how dare they go and leave us alone! They may be angry with other people – how dare they have mothers, fathers, grandparents! They may simply be angry with life – how dare the sun be shining when I am so unhappy!

Guilt

There are many reasons why a child might feel guilty. Perhaps he or she feels they were naughty the last time they saw the person who has since died; perhaps they think they should have been able to say goodbye to them.

Just like the child who is abused or abandoned, the child who is still young when one or both of their parents dies will subconsciously feel that it was *their* fault, whatever logic may tell them. Having been convinced in their young mind that their mother and father were wonderful people who could do no wrong, if one of those wonderful people suddenly disappears from the scene – whatever the reason – the child's subconscious mind will tell him or her that it must be because they weren't lovable enough for them to stay around. Research has shown that many of those who were very young children during the war – when father may have disappeared for years (if not for ever) through no choice of his own – have grown up to have a very low self-esteem. They may be able to reason that the fact that father was conscripted into the armed forces and went to Europe had nothing at all to do with how lovable his children were – but the subconscious damage has been done none the less.

Many children will also feel guilty – as will most adults – the first time they realize that they are happy or laughing or have temporarily forgotten the dead person. But it should be explained to them that this too is normal and right, and that it does not mean that they didn't really love the one they have lost. He or she needs to be reassured that, because the person who has died really loved them, they would want them to be happy again and to enjoy life.

Lack of understanding

Because by the time we are adult, whether or not we have personal experience of bereavement, we know a certain amount about death and have had time to form our own views about it, it is easy to forget that, for the child whose first encounter with death it may be, the entire concept is usually difficult to grasp. In their young lives the people who have gone out of the door have always come back again sooner or later. Not only do they have to become accustomed to the idea that someone will *never* return, but they will have to form some opinion of where they have gone. Such opinions will naturally be strongly influenced by the beliefs of those closest to them.

Unfortunately, particularly in Britain, a great deal of emphasis is often placed on keeping up appearances even in times of tragedy. It is considered almost a virtue to withhold one's tears. 'She's being so brave and coping wonderfully well – she even managed not to cry at the funeral.' Not only does such behaviour dramatically prolong the period of grieving, but it can have terrible long-term effects upon the physical and emotional health of the individual. Just as every adult should be allowed to cry, so every child should not only be allowed but should actually be encouraged to do so. If they feel unhappy then they must show it; this is not a time to be 'brave'. And boys have just as much right to tears as girls. It is only sensible to have a word with friends or teachers so that, should the child dissolve into tears for no apparent reason, they will be sympathetic and understanding.

It is equally important that you allow your child to see you crying too. He or she should grow up realizing that you are a warm human being, with a human reaction to sorrowful events. If you succeed in hiding your tears from them, they may begin to believe that you do not really care and this belief could colour their entire future relationship with you. Grief can often bring people very close together, so allow your child to comfort you in the same way that you attempt to comfort them.

Talk to your child about the feelings you are both likely to have in this time of grief. Explain that all the emotions they are likely to experience are normal and that there is nothing to feel guilty or ashamed about. Reassure them that, if there is anything they want to discuss with you, you will always be ready. Let them know how you are feeling and allow them to comfort you – this will in fact be really beneficial to you both.

Talk to him or her about death in general and what it means. Remember, however, to use terms of reference they will understand (which will depend upon their age and experience). If the death has come at the end of a long illness, you might wish to try and explain that it is perhaps a blessing for the person who has died as they no longer have to suffer. But do remember to reassure the child that most people recover from illnesses and accidents, so they don't panic if they are ill later.

Don't try to pretend that the person who has died never existed. Talk about them. They can still be a part of your lives, although in a different way. 'Daddy would have liked this' or 'Grannie would have enjoyed that' gives the child a sense of continuity and lessens the feeling of abandonment they might otherwise experience. If you have always kept photographs of happier times around the house, let them remain in place so that the child does not feel that everything to do with the person who has died has to be removed from the scene.

Whatever your religious beliefs, many children derive a great deal of comfort from the thought that the person who has died is still around in some way and not just buried under the ground. Using language understandable to the child and that doesn't conflict with your own convictions, try and reassure them that the one they feel they have lost is not really so very far away, but still cares for them and watches over them lovingly and protectively. If the child wishes to talk to the person who has died, let them do so, explaining that the words will be heard although they won't be able to hear the reply in the normal way. Many children find it reassuring, particularly after the death of a parent, still to be able to tell Mummy or Daddy about what has happened that day. Take care, however, that you do not describe the situation in such a way that it alarms the child.

Jenny's beloved Grandpa died when the little girl was six. Because he had lived just down the street from her own home, Jenny had seen a great deal of her grandfather and so she missed him intensely. Having been brought up in a family with strong religious convictions, she was quite able to accept her mother's explanation that Grandpa had gone to be with God. She was also comforted to know that, because he loved his little granddaughter so much, her grandfather would watch over her and look after her.

Shortly afterwards, however – and for the first time in her young life – Jenny began to exhibit many of the signs of stress and anxiety. Her parents were unable to understand the reason for this. They didn't think it could be connected with the death of her grandfather, as she had been through all the usual stages of grief and seemed to have come to terms with her loss. Now she appeared tense and anxious and far more inhibited in her behaviour than previously.

Eventually, they found that Jenny had taken the idea of grandfather watching over her so literally that she felt his eyes were always on her. She was frightened to do anything in case Grandpa thought she was being naughty; she did not like to appear too happy in case he felt that she was no longer sorry about his death. Once they understood the situation, Jenny's parents were able to explain to her that, even though Grandpa was near enough to hear if she spoke to him, he was no more likely to be with her all the time than he had been when he was alive and lived down the road. But you see how easy it is – however good your intentions – to cause anxiety in the mind of a child.

Any child of four or older is old enough to be allowed to attend whatever form of service or ceremony you might have, although it is obviously essential that they understand why you are all there and what is happening. Once again, all explanations must of necessity be made with regard to his or her own level of comprehension. The finality of the ceremony, whether it be a cremation or a burial, is to the child almost like saying goodbye to the person they have lost – and this is as necessary to them as it is to any adult. You should tell them that it will be an emotional experience, there will be others there too and many people may feel like crying, but this is normal and just a way of showing how sorry they are that the person is dead. He or she must know that they can cry too, if they feel the need, and that no-one will criticize them or think that they are behaving like a baby. Keep your explanations as simple as possible, but do be honest with your child at all times.

While you certainly should not destroy all evidence of the person who has died, particularly if it is a parent, be careful that you do not unwittingly cause confusion in the child's mind.

Maria was naturally very distressed when her husband suffered a massive heart attack comparatively young. When he died a few hours later, leaving her with three young children, she determined that everything in the home would continue to look as if he were still living there. So his pipe and a box of matches were left on the coffee table in the sitting room, his raincoat still hung on the hook in the hall, the book he had been reading remained on the dresser. It was just as though he were about to walk through the door at any moment. All this was very disconcerting for the children, who were having enough difficulty in accepting their father's death. On the one hand they were being told that he would not be coming back any more; yet on the other all his possessions were lying around the house waiting for him to use them again. There comes a time, hard as it may be, when clothes and personal possessions have to be packed away and the family has to establish for itself a new and different routine.

One of my patients told me that her own mother had continued to put out clean clothes for her father for years after he had died and that she, the child, had been terrified to go into what had been her parents' bedroom in case her father suddenly appeared as a ghost to dress in those clothes.

All anniversaries are difficult to deal with for the first year.

Whether it is a birthday, Christmas, Mother's Day, the child's birthday or even the school Open Day, the child will be extremely conscious of the fact that one special person is missing. Naturally these will be emotional times for adult and child, but this is only to be expected. After the first year, however, it should be somewhat less emotionally draining. This does not mean that you cannot remember the person who has died on all these 'special' days, but try and keep a sense of proportion for your child's sake. It is far better to say 'Let's take a bunch of flowers and put them on Granny's grave for Christmas' than to sob over the turkey because the old lady is no longer there in person.

Whether you take your child to visit a grave or a memorial stone depends very much on your own beliefs and also on the child's wishes. If you are someone who chooses to go regularly (whether this means weekly or annually), give the child the opportunity to accompany you, but never force them to do so. Some young children find it difficult to come to terms with the fact that someone they knew and loved is actually buried beneath the ground; if so, they should not be compelled to visit the site of a grave unless and until they feel ready to do so. Other children find that they are able to feel closer to the one they have lost when they are beside a grave, and this often brings feelings of peace and consolation. Remember that visiting a cemetery does not have to be a morbid or unhappy occasion – it is more a mark of respect and a continuing link with the person who has died. The child should be encouraged to talk quietly but normally and should not feel that there is something wrong with them if, after the first few occasions, they do not feel the need to cry or to be unhappy.

A friend of mine who was ten when her mother died tells me that, throughout her teenage years – the time when a daughter most needs her mother – she would go and sit on the grass beside her mother's grave and talk to her, telling her about all her hopes and fears and discussing all her adolescent problems just as though her mother were sitting there beside her. Although, naturally, she was never able to receive a verbal reply, nonetheless she felt better just for having talked to someone who she was – and still is – convinced cared for her and could hear every word.

Many children, particularly older ones, feel a great need to visit the place where the death took place – especially if it was a parent who died. This is not a morbid or masochistic desire on their part, but rather a way of acknowledging the reality of the situation. Of course many adults feel this too, which is why those whose loved ones have died in battles or in other disasters often make long and difficult journeys to visit the scene. As with visiting a grave, seeing the place where the death occurred should neither be forced upon the child nor forbidden if they express a desire to do it.

As time begins to heal the open sores of grief, it is only natural for the child to become happy again and to return to living a normal life. Yet many of them are suddenly struck by pangs of guilt when this begins to happen and they realize that they are no longer thinking constantly about the person who has died. This is why talking is so important – it is the only way the child can be made to understand that it is right and natural for life to go on and for people to be happy again. It does not mean that they don't miss the one they have lost; it is simply a part of life's natural healing process.

The death of a brother or sister – particularly if near their own age – can provoke traumatic reactions in a child. If the death resulted from an illness, they may begin to develop psychosomatic symptoms. Suddenly having realized that death can happen to someone of their own generation and is not the prerogative of old people, they may become frightened that it will happen to them too. Although there is no harm at all in allowing them to see your grief, emphasize to them that this emotion is something you have in common, so that they don't begin to think that you wish they had died instead of their brother or sister.

Pets can play a vitally important role in a child's life and he or she can be deeply affected by the death of an animal, whether a cat, a dog, a rabbit or even a mouse. They must therefore be allowed to pass through all the stages of grieving for an animal just as they would for a person. Because the lifespan of a small animal is normally far shorter than that of a human, the emotions a child experiences when one of them dies can actually help to prepare him or her for the feelings they will have when they lose someone close to them later in life. Children brought up on farms have always found it far easier to come to terms with birth and death because for them it has been a regular and natural occurrence.

If a pet becomes ill and has to be humanely destroyed by a vet, tell the child first – provided they are old enough to understand – so that they can say goodbye to their friend. Distressing as this may be, it is far worse for them to come home to find that the beloved animal is no longer there. Allow them to cry and give them ample time to grieve. Only when the child is ready should he or she be given a new pet; that animal should be a joy in its own right rather than a 'replacement' for the pet they have lost. To a child, the thought that one dog can 'replace' another is as abhorrent as it is for a mother to think that having a new baby 'replaces' one she has lost.

Death is never an easy matter to deal with, whether for adult or child, but the way you cope with it may well dramatically affect your child's attitudes and emotions when faced with the situation in the future.

Checklist

- Remember that your child will be experiencing similar emotions to your own – but will not understand them. Talk to them about your loss, using words and terminology appropriate for their age and intelligence.
- Assure them that death is not some kind of divine punishment for bad behaviour.
- Allow your child to take part in the mourning. Let them talk, cry and ask questions.
- Don't send them away unless absolutely essential. Whatever happens, never try to pretend that the death hasn't happened.
- Allow them to go through all the stages of grief: unhappiness, fear, loneliness, anger, guilt and lack of understanding.
- Let them cry as much as they need; and allow them to see you cry too.
- Discuss your feelings, and theirs; allow them to comfort you just as you try to comfort them.
- Talk about death in general terms. Reassure them that it isn't the inevitable result of every illness.
- Talk about the person who has died in as natural a way as possible.
- Let them know that the one they have lost is still near and still cares for them, even though they cannot see them.
- Provided he or she is old enough to understand what is

happening, allow your child to be present at whatever type of service or ceremony may take place. Explain to them in advance what will happen there.

- Don't remove all evidence of the existence of the one who has died; on the other hand, don't be tempted to make your home into a type of 'shrine' or leave items around that would indicate that they are likely to walk through the door at any moment.
- Encourage your child to remember anniversaries and so on, but not in a morbid or grief-stricken way.
- A cemetery should be visited as and when the child wishes it – neither force nor forbid them to do so.
- If they express a desire to see the scene of death, then – if it is practicable – they should be allowed to do so.
- Reassure them that there is nothing wrong in starting to feel happy again and beginning to live life normally.
- If his or her brother or sister has died, allow your child to share your grief. Watch for psychosomatic symptoms and never say anything that could lead them to believe that you wish they had gone instead.
- Remember that children really love their pets and allow them to grieve for an animal in the same way as for a human. Give them time to say goodbye if appropriate and, if you give them another pet, do not imply that it is a replacement for the one they have lost.

5

Problems at School

Very few people would agree with the old saying that 'schooldays are the happiest days of your life', although some people will obviously have found them enjoyable. Others would say that they tolerated, rather than enjoyed, their time at school, while many will tell you that they found the whole experience miserable or even traumatic. Psychological research tells us that many of the most stressful periods in a child's life are, in fact, associated with school. In his book, *Helping Your Anxious Child*, Dr David Lewis says:

The four periods of your child's life when stress is likely to be at its greatest are:
1. Starting school, and making that big change from being with you all day to adjusting to a new routine.
2. Changing schools, and having to make friends – especially the move from primary to secondary education.
3. In the fifth year of second education while revising for exams.
4. Around puberty, when mind and body are coming to terms with different ways of feeling and responding.

Other aspects of school life that can also cause stress in children are:

1. Excessive or unrealistic expectations of performance – whether by parents, teachers or the child himself or herself.
2. Bullying by other children or even by certain teachers.
3. Experiencing learning difficulties in ways that often go unnoticed by others.
4. Superior ability to such a marked degree that the child is isolated from his or her peers.

There are many ways in which a caring adult can help to alleviate what may produce at best a general anxiety on the part of the child and at worst a school phobia where he or she is so psychologically distressed that the prospect of even entering the school gates is sufficient to induce terrifying panic attacks.

Starting school

Although it is not compulsory for a child to start school until the age of five, many now attend some kind of playschool, usually for half a day. Such playschools have many benefits; they are an excellent way of introducing the child to the fact that their mother will regularly leave them in the care of others but will always return to collect them at a particular time. Playschool also provides a good opportunity for the child to mix with others of their own age and to be one of a crowd instead of the centre of attention – this is particularly important if they are an only child and used to the constant care of a single adult.

Children as young as three can be ready for playschool – but it is extremely important that the time at which they start does not coincide with the birth of a new baby in the family. It may often seem to the parents to be a practical solution, allowing the mother to have the mornings free to be with her baby and then to spend time with the small child in the afternoons, but the child will see it as a form of rejection, believing that their parents are sending them out of the way now there is a new baby to love.

There are several ways in which you can help to prepare your children for learning before they start school; they don't even have to know that this is what you are doing. It matters less that you try and teach them to read and write than that you encourage them to become as independent as possible, so that they feel in control of the situation when they enter the school. Make sure that they can dress themselves (thank goodness for elasticated waistbands, velcro and slip-on shoes!). See that they know how to use the toilet alone and that they are not too inhibited to ask if they need to.

There are many ways in which young children can be encouraged to use their brains. Spend time together, either looking at books or actually reading to them. In this way they will become used to the feel of books and to the concept that the squiggles on the page really *mean* something. They will accept which way the pages turn and that we read the lines from left to right. If they show a desire to learn the sounds associated with the letters of the alphabet, then by all means encourage and teach them. Never force knowledge upon them, however, as this will merely set up a stubborn resistance that may be difficult to eradicate. Games such as 'I Spy' are often helpful, as they will find them fun and will also begin to associate the sounds of the letters with actual objects, thus removing reading from the abstract to the factual.

Ensuring that your children have a plentiful supply of drawing materials – chalk, blackboard, pencils, crayons and paper on which to scribble –- is more important than trying to teach them to write. Let them get used to the feel of holding those writing implements and of transferring marks on to paper so that, when they do go to school and have more formal lessons, they will not feel uncomfortable or unhappy. If he or she shows a real desire to copy letters then they should be allowed to do so – and many children do like to learn how to write their own names – but, once again, the pace should be set by them and never be forced by an eager adult, anxious that their child will have a head start on everyone else. Remember that when it comes to the way in which they hold a pencil, wrong habits learned at a very early age are extremely difficult to break.

It is perhaps best to resist the temptation to teach your children arithmetic before they start school, as the way this subject is taught can change and every school has its own particular method of teaching. But you can help them to become familiar with the numbers themselves, encouraging them to count (whether fingers, the stairs or sweets). Other ways you can help them to associate numbers with reality is by allowing them to share out objects (one for you, one for me and one for baby) or to count the number of steps it takes to cross the room or the number of biscuits left on the plate.

The school–home link

Be as supportive as possible when your child makes that giant stride from home to school. In the early days they will probably bring home drawings or objects they have made in class and, if you are to nurture their confidence and belief in themselves, praise their work and find a place in your home to display it. Be prepared to spend time with them, listening to their attempts at reading or reciting tables. Remember to be patient if progress appears to you to be slow – their brain is working very hard to acquire so much new knowledge all at the same time. Try and resist the temptation to impose your methods on them, even if you do think they are superior to the ones used by the class teacher. You will simply confuse them and they won't know whose method to accept.

There is now much more communication between parents and teachers than there used to be. Many of today's adults were brought up in more restrictive times, when their own parents were somewhat diffident about approaching the school. However, present-day teachers, particularly those in infant and junior schools, actively encourage such contact. It is also important that the teacher is informed should your child have any particular emotional problems at home or be experiencing difficulty with the work they have been asked to do.

Homework

Once your child reaches the age where homework is set, it is essential to establish a routine right from the outset. Habits formed now will prepare them for periods of more intensive study in the future.

Discuss a possible routine with your child so that he or she feels they have some say in the pattern of their life. This will achieve far more satisfactory results – and will avoid feelings of resentment in the child him or herself – than merely imposing your own wishes upon them. You may wish to make suggestions, such as recommending that they do their homework as soon as they come in from school so that they know they have the rest of the time before bed to play with friends, watch television or generally relax, but remember that your ideas are far more likely to be accepted if they are put as suggestions. You are dealing with a child who is becoming more and more aware of his or her growing independence, and they will want to have some say in the routine of their own life.

Let your child know that you care about what they are doing by asking them what homework he or she has (many older children actually have a homework timetable) and listening to tables, spellings, etc. Give them a suitable spot in which they can do their work away from family distractions. Children are often hesitant to speak up in class, so he or she may well ask you about some problem that arises from their homework. If you don't know the answer, say so (after all, they will have to learn soon enough that you are only human) and make suggestions as to where they can look for help.

Perhaps you could ask about what he or she did in class, so that they will be able to work out a solution for themselves. Reassure them that they are not expected to know everything – there would be no point in going to school – and that they shouldn't be nervous about asking the teacher; it is certainly far better than plodding on and possibly basing future work on a false assumption.

Some parents feel that their children are given too much homework, whereas others will insist that the amount is too small. Provided your child is making adequate progress compared to the others in their class, there is probably nothing to worry about. If, however, they are given so much work that they cannot cope and become distressed, try to find out whether the teacher has in fact set an unrealistic amount or whether your child is merely over-conscientious.

Changing schools

Changing schools and giving up what has become a comfortable routine for something totally unknown can be a most traumatic time for any child. If the change is from primary to secondary education, it is quite likely that he or she will be making that move in the company of several friends and so the change will be less difficult. Sometimes, however, it is necessary for the child to make the move alone; perhaps there is a particular reason why another school is thought to be preferable or perhaps the family is moving from one part of the country to another. At such times you will need to be very caring and supportive if your child is not to find the situation extremely stressful.

There are, however, ways in which you can help your child through this difficult time.

- Contact the new school and see whether it is possible to arrange for your child to meet someone who is going to be in the same class, so that they will not feel completely alone on that frightening first day.
- Take advantage of the assistance offered by many schools and let your child be shown around the premises before they start there. It will help to lessen the feeling of strangeness if they at least know their way around the building.

- Try and find out from the school in advance as many details as possible about books, items of uniform or sports equipment.
- Ensure that your child's home life is as settled and as stable as possible, especially if you have just moved home – an event that is traumatic in itself and that causes considerable upheaval in everyone's life.

Exams

Tests and examinations are stressful and difficult at whatever age they occur. And of course children at school tend to make each other feel worse by constantly reacknowledging their fears and dreads both of the examinations themselves and the possible results. You can be a great help to your child at such times.

- Keep home life as free from tension as possible. This is not the time to be over-critical about hairstyle, taste in music or tidiness of bedroom.
- Make sure your child's lifestyle is as healthy as possible, as this will help them to resist stress-related physical problems. See that they have regular meals and don't simply reach for a bun or some biscuits while studying. Try to ensure that he or she has enough sleep; however much they may wish to continue revising, there comes a point when the brain will not assimilate any more knowledge and where more benefit is to be gained from going to bed. Persuade them to relax by spending some time doing things that have nothing to do with school work.
- Discuss their revision programme with them and try to convince them that they should follow a regular routine rather than leave everything to the last minute. Accept that they are entitled to time for things other than work.
- Let them know that you support them and that, provided they put in the appropriate amount of work, you will not be over-critical should the results not be as wonderful as they would wish.
- Where work done at home on projects counts towards final results, don't try to 'help' by doing the work for them, but do be supportive and perhaps spend time discussing the projects, or suggesting works of reference or sources of information.

- Make time for them so that they know you are on their side at what is a difficult time.

16 plus

This is a difficult time for any teenager, even before you take into account problems to do with school and further education. Even those who decide that they wish to stay on at school or continue their education at a sixth-form college – and possibly progress to university – find it difficult when they see others of their own age leaving school, getting jobs and having money to spend (and free time in which to spend it) without the restrictions of homework and studying for exams. These factors, combined with natural feelings of restlessness, make it very hard for a teenager to feel settled and content, even when they know they will be able to achieve more in the long term. Their need for a caring, supportive adult and a stable home life is even more accentuated at such a time.

Your son or daughter will have to contend with other problems in their life at this age. Changes will be taking place in both their physical and emotional states, and some teenagers find this easier to deal with than others.

Interests other than school are vital at such a time, as they will need outlets for their energy and enthusiasm and a chance to meet others of their own age away from a school environment. Friends are very important to a teenager and can often seem to them to be more supportive than their own family.

Excessive expectations

A considerable amount of stress is caused when a child feels that he or she is being placed under pressure because of the hopes and desires of others. This is so whether a teacher is pushing them too hard or they feel that their parents have hopes that they know are beyond their capabilities.

When Sophie started going to the local secondary school at eleven years old, her sister Rachel had already been there for three years. Both girls were bright and intelligent, although from the beginning Sophie had found learning easier than her sister. Rachel, however, had always worked hard at her studies and was doing quite well. Because they both attended the same school, it followed that the girls frequently were taught by the same teacher. One unenlightened teacher foolishly began to tell Rachel that her younger sister was doing better than she was. Perhaps he thought that this would spur Rachel on to greater things, but he could not have been more wrong. Once she realized that, however hard she worked, her marks would never compare with those of her sister, Rachel simply gave up trying. Sadly this lack of effort carried through into every subject and Rachel eventually left school with no qualifications at all, even though, had she continued working, her results would probably have been above average.

Danny, on the other hand, was one of those children who would never find academic work easy – although he was by no means unintelligent. Like Rachel, he too put in a great deal of work and tried his very best to do well. Danny always found scientific subjects particularly difficult and, even after doing the best he could, he received low marks in test after test. The science teacher at his school refused to believe that Danny had made any effort at all and accused him of idling his time away instead of working. After this accusation had been hurled at him several times, usually in front of other members of his class, Danny simply decided working was pointless if no-one was prepared to believe he had made the effort.

Many problems arise when one parent desperately wants his or her child to follow in their own footsteps; or, even worse, when he or she simply assumes that they will. 'Of course he is going to be an accountant, just like his father' or 'Oh well, he is bound to go into the family firm' have caused many a child to suffer from stress. On the one hand he or she wants to please their parents and not to disappoint them; but on the other they know perfectly well that they either are not suited to a particular job or profession, or simply don't want it.

Other parents may try to live their lives through their children. Arthur and Gwen had both come from very poor families. They had worked hard all their lives and had reached a stage where they had a better standard of living than their parents could ever have dreamed of. They wanted even greater things for their own two children; in particular, the opportunity for the type of further education they had never had. The fact that their children had no desire to continue studying did not even enter their heads.

Heather, Arthur and Gwen's daughter and the elder of the children, was quite a strong character, and she refused absolutely to continue with her education. She left school at 16 and began work in a London department store. Because, although she had never been particularly academic, Heather was an intelligent young woman, she progressed well in her working environment, eventually becoming a buyer in the fashion department – a career that enabled her to travel the world and brought her both personal satisfaction and financial reward.

Garry, on the other hand, was meeker than his older sister. Although he had no particular desire to continue his studies, he did not like to upset his parents and worked hard at school, just managing to obtain a university place. Once there, however, he found the work and the amount of private study was too much for him and, after 15 months, he collapsed from nervous exhaustion and was forced to leave.

Each child is a complete individual, and should never have to feel that they must conform to someone else's idea of what their future should be. The stress caused by being pulled in so many directions can have an effect on their life long after their period of education has ended.

Bullying

Bullying can take many different forms, but in every case it causes stress and anxiety to the recipient. It may involve physical violence – this does not refer to two boys scrapping in the school playground but to persistent ill-treatment where there is a perpetrator and a victim. It could also be name-calling, ignoring, or stealing or hiding of possessions. Even if these seem comparatively trivial offences, the pain and anguish they cause can create problems lasting a lifetime.

Bullying knows no boundaries of sex or age. It can occur at any stage, from the nursery school child to the teenager, and girls can be just as guilty as boys. Most victims are those children who, for whatever reason, have a diminished self-esteem. Perhaps they are the ones at home for whom no-one seems to have any time; perhaps their ears stick out or they have a stammer; perhaps they have a 'different' name; perhaps they are bad at sports; or perhaps their only offence is that they are new to the district. Whatever the original cause of the problem, bullying creates its own vicious circle as the timid child becomes even more frightened and timid, and therefore even more likely to be picked on.

No-one seems to talk about bullying – neither the perpetrator nor the victim – so it is up to caring adults to watch for signs. Some of the more common indications that a child is being bullied are:

reluctance to go to school;
the child suddenly becoming quiet and withdrawn at home;
the onset of phantom symptoms of illness;
any of the symptoms of stress described in Part One.

If you think that your child is being bullied at school, you will have to try a little gentle probing. It is usually a mistake to come straight out and ask: 'Are you being bullied?' as most children will immediately become defensive and deny the suggestion. Try talking generally about the day at school, asking what he or she has done, who their friends are, what games they played at break-time, and so on.

Should you find that your child is indeed the victim of a school bully, there are several things you can do.

- Tell the school at once, as it is vitally important that the bullying is stopped. If, as is likely, your child begs you to say nothing, promise that you will ask the teacher not to say that you have spoken to them. Most teachers are quite adept at putting an end to this sort of situation once it is brought to their attention. If you feel that the school is not doing enough to prevent bullying, you can approach the Board of Governors, which will include parents among its members.
- Be particularly loving and sympathetic towards your child. Let them know that you understand what they are going through and that they can talk to you at any time.
- There is no point in simply telling your child to 'hit them back'. The timid child will not be able to do so and, apart from the fact that they could be hurt, they might be humiliated further by being easily defeated.
- Try and boost his or her confidence in other areas of their life.

71

Perhaps they could be encouraged to join a club or interest group outside school, where they would meet different people – people who don't automatically think of them as a bully's victim – and this might well help to raise their level of self-esteem.

If it is distressing to find that your child is the victim of the school bully, think how devastating it must be to discover that your much-loved son or daughter is the one doing the bullying. Of course sometimes the child is merely copying behaviour they see at home, where they themselves may be the object of victimization, whether perpetrated by a brother or sister – or even by a parent. But in many cases the parents of the school bully are kind and caring people who have no conception of the way in which their child is behaving. Upsetting as it may be when a teacher or another parent informs you about your child's actions, if he or she is terrorizing another child you have to do something about it, for both their sakes.

- There is little point in giving him or her a taste of their own medicine and attempting to 'beat it out of them'. All you will be doing is encouraging them to accept that it is all right to inflict deliberate pain on another person.
- Much as you may feel like shouting at them, try and talk reasonably to your child. Explain to them how cruel it is to hurt someone else – whether physically or mentally – and ask them to imagine what it must feel like to be on the receiving end. Emphasize that it is only weak people who need to bully, as strong people don't have anything to prove. Make sure they know that bullying is something you simply will not tolerate.
- Ask them to think of a way in which they can make amends to the former victim. Perhaps they can apologize. Perhaps, if the other child is particularly timid, they can take him or her under their wing and be protective towards them.
- Keep in touch with his or her form teacher and ask to be kept informed of your child's behaviour and as to whether or not the bullying stops. When it does end, let your child know that you are pleased with them for having stopped.
- Ask yourself just why your child has reached the stage where they have had to victimize another person. The bully is someone who feels the need to be the centre of attention owing to a lack of

self-confidence. What can you do to help boost his or her opinion of themselves?
- Consider whether the school bully is in fact the victim of bullying at home and is getting their own back on another child who is weaker than him or herself. It is easy for parents who have several children – particularly if they are close in age – not to realize that one of them is being picked on by his or her brothers or sisters.

Learning difficulties

There may be many reasons why a child develops learning difficulties. Perhaps ill health caused them to miss some early schooling and they have never been able to catch up. Perhaps they have had to change schools to one where the teaching system is different, and the change has caused them to take a backward step in their ability to learn. Perhaps your child is one of the more timid ones who is afraid to ask questions in front of the other children and so, having failed to understand some of the early work, has found anything based on that work totally confusing. There can also be physical problems that may not be immediately apparent.

The teacher in the junior school that Lisa attended liked to keep what she called 'her trouble-makers' at the front of the class and right under her eye. Because Lisa did not fit into this category, she was assigned a seat near the back of the room.

As the terms went on it became obvious that Lisa was making very slow progress compared to the other children and, the teacher having 30 children in her class and not being able to give Lisa much in the way of personal attention, the child was left to muddle along as best she could. By the time she was nine it became obvious that Lisa could no longer cope in a normal class, and parents and teachers agreed that she should attend special remedial classes. If she didn't do sufficiently well in these, they would have to consider sending her to a school for educationally subnormal children. It did not take the remedial teacher long to discover that Lisa was in fact a bright little girl but that she didn't always hear clearly what was said to her. She could cope well enough in a one-to-one situation or in the home environment, but sitting at the back of a class of noisy children she had missed a great deal of what the teacher had said.

73

All it took was for Lisa to be given a hearing aid and she was as able as any of the other children in the class. Sadly, however, she had virtually missed the first four years of her primary school education and it took a great deal of private coaching before she was able to catch up.

It is easy, of course, for a parent to recognize severe deafness or shortsightedness in their child, but it may be far more difficult to observe a slight defect. That defect may not interfere in any way with the child's everyday life but may be more than enough to present them with many problems at school, particularly if he or she finds themselves one of a noisy crowd and sitting at some distance from the teacher and the blackboard.

Children, like adults, vary dramatically in their personalities. One child, when faced with difficulties, will become even more determined to overcome them and will do everything in his or her power to do so. Another may feel that, if they have tried and are unable to succeed, they might just as well give up and stop trying. Researchers have found that many of those children who have later been diagnosed as having learning difficulties were simply children who found early school work confusing and, feeling that the struggle was pointless, gave up completely.

Dyslexia, of course, is a separate problem. It is a complaint that is known to affect about one in ten of the population and is more prevalent among boys than girls. It has nothing to do with the child's intelligence; indeed many of today's famous and successful people are dyslexic. If you can recognize dyslexia in your child at an early stage, there is a great deal that can be done to help them. Here are some of the tell-tale signs:

difficulty in reading words in sequence;
a tendency to reverse words ('saw' instead of 'was' or 'tar' instead of 'rat');
a habit of writing letters or figures back to front;
difficulty in telling the time from a clock;
they find sequences hard to remember (days of the week, months of the year, etc.);
an obvious contrast between the child's lack of ability in reading and writing skills and their talents in other areas.

Of course, recognition of a problem is not in itself a cure. However, once you realize that your child is dyslexic – and, even more importantly, once *they* realize it – a lot of pressure is removed from you both; you know that he or she is not lazy or unintelligent. Many dyslexics can be helped by special visiting teachers or at local literacy centres. Further information can be obtained from the British Dyslexia Association (see Appendix).

Gifted children

In their own way, gifted children can find themselves faced with as many problems as children with learning difficulties. They often feel that they do not 'fit in' or 'belong' with their classmates. They can appear to be in a 'no-win' situation: if they remain in a class with their contemporaries they may become frustrated, jealous, mischievous or bored, but if they are promoted to a higher class where they may find the work stimulating, they will not be able to fit in socially with their much older classmates.

Many gifted children grow up to feel that they do not belong anywhere, and they are frequently victims of school bullies – who may well be far less able students and jealous of their ability.

How can you help your gifted child?

- If you feel that he or she is more than just 'bright' and is truly gifted in some academic way, it may be worth making inquiries about the special schools that exist for such children.
- However talented they may be in one direction, try and encourage other interests so that they don't become too one-sided.
- If he or she is particularly gifted in one specific subject, try and resist the tendency to force them to concentrate on that subject so that they develop even more dramatically. Tempting as it may be to have your child classed as a 'genius', such children are rarely happy – and surely a happy and fulfilled childhood is what we all want for our sons and daughters.
- Encourage them to find other outlets and challenges for their brain.

While your child is of school age he or she will demand not just your understanding but your time. We all appreciate that time is a precious commodity indeed, particularly when both parents are working outside the home. However, time given to a school-age child can lay the foundations for self-confidence and peace of mind in the present and in the future.

Checklist

Starting school

- If sending them to playschool, make sure the timing does not coincide with the arrival of a new baby.
- Make sure your child can dress him or herself and use the toilet.
- Spend time looking at books with them.
- Give them the tools with which to draw and colour.
- Only try to teach them to read if they really want to learn.
- Allow them to become familiar with numbers rather than trying to teach them arithmetic.

School–home link

- Be patient and supportive.
- Let them do things the teacher's way rather than yours.
- Communicate with their teacher. See that he or she knows if there are any problems at home that could affect the child emotionally.

Homework

- Help your child to establish a regular homework routine – allow them to choose it for themselves if possible.
- Show an interest in the work set for home study.
- Make time to hear spellings, tables, etc.
- Find them a quiet spot in which to work.
- If they can't cope with the amount, speak to the teacher to find out the cause.

Changing schools

- Ask the school if it is possible for your child to meet another pupil before starting school.
- Arrange for them to see round the school in advance, so they are familiar with it.

- Find out in advance about uniform, sports equipment, books, etc.

Exams

- Make sure his or her lifestyle is as healthy as possible during revision and exam time.
- Help your child to plan a revision routine rather than leave everything to the last minute.
- Keep home life as free from tension as possible.

16 plus

- Be supportive at a time of emotional and physical changes.
- Understand their frustrations if they see others of their own age getting jobs, and having money and freedom.
- Encourage them to have other outlets and friends apart from those at school.

Expectations

- Don't expect your child to follow in your footsteps unless they want to do so.
- If they stop working, find out whether they are being compared unfavourably to a brother or sister.
- You may wish your child to continue with further education, but don't make them if they aren't suited to it.

Bullying

If you think your child is being bullied:

- Ask indirect questions to see if this is so.
- Report the matter to the school immediately.
- Be loving and supportive towards your child.
- Don't simply tell them to 'hit back'.
- Try and boost their confidence in other areas. Encourage them to join clubs or make new friends away from school.

If you think your child is the bully:

- Never hope to cure the situation by giving them 'a taste of their own medicine'.

- Talk to them, making it clear that you will not tolerate bullying.
- Encourage them to see things from the victim's point of view, and remind them that only the weak need to inflict pain upon others.
- Ask them to think of a way of making amends. Encourage them to be protective towards their former victim.
- Keep in touch with the teacher, and ask to be kept informed.
- Ask yourself why your child needs to bully others. Are they themselves being bullied at home?

Learning difficulties

- Ensure that your child doesn't have a hearing or sight problem.
- Keep an eye on their progress so that difficulties can be recognized as early as possible.
- Encourage them to feel confident in as many areas of life as possible.
- Check to see whether dyslexia could be the cause and, if so, see that they have help at a very early stage.

Gifted children

- If your child is especially gifted, make enquiries about special schools.
- Don't try to force them to become a tunnel-visioned 'genius'.
- Keep an eye on their behaviour and treatment at school.
- Always encourage them to have as many different interests as possible.

In all areas

- Give your school-age child as much of your time as you can at this vitally important time of their life.

6

Outside Influences

Like it or not, we are all influenced to some extent by those around us and by the media. This is simply an extension of our earlier programming – although hopefully, as we mature, we find that we can control a greater part of the effect that these outside influences have upon us and upon the way in which we conduct our lives.

Children, however, find it extremely difficult to detach themselves from such external pressures. Having started out by absorbing many of their parents' values and ideals, they then go on to enlarge that sphere of influence to incorporate the ideas of teachers and friends of their own age as well as concepts presented to them by television and radio. And, of course, any child hates to be the one who is 'different'; mostly they are far more comfortable when they are able to conform and fit in with their peer group. Indeed, it is only the strongest-willed child who can find the courage to break away from what is considered 'normal' within their own particular environment. This remains true even when such conformity leads them into circumstances that, if this pressure did not exist, they would prefer to avoid: such as smoking, stealing, early sexual experimentation, or drug, solvent and alcohol abuse. The parent or other caring adult has therefore to be ever-watchful if they are to recognize these external pressures and help the child to avoid the problems they can cause.

Situations that can arise from 'people pressure'

Stealing

There must be very few people who have not been guilty of stealing of one sort or another at some time in their lives – although most would hotly deny the allegation. But try asking yourself the following questions.

Do I try and find ways, however small, of avoiding income tax?

Do I do my best to get out of paying a parking fine?

If the checkout girl at the local supermarket accidentally hands

79

me too much change, do I pocket the excess, telling myself that such a large organization will never notice the difference?

When making an insurance claim, have I ever over-estimated the value of the goods lost, reasoning that I had been paying premiums for years so the company was still making a profit out of me?

Do I make as many personal telephone calls as possible from the office?

I do not quote these examples to make judgments – but if you answer yes to these, or any similar questions, think about the basic example you are setting your child. You probably don't consider that any of the above situations involves you in stealing; after all, everyone does it, don't they? Remember, however, that children are highly observant and if they come to accept as normal such behaviour by one or both of their parents, they are more likely to be predisposed to accept the concept of dishonesty.

To see the effect our lifestyle has upon our children, we have only to read a recent Home Office report that shows that most young people now consider that the theft of five-pounds-worth of goods from a shop is a trivial offence, as is fiddling the Social Security. Indeed, many of them feel the same about stealing a car: it is thought to be more an example of high spirits than a crime.

Andrew's father ran his own business, and when the little boy was still quite small he would hear his parents discussing the company at the dinner table. His father would proudly tell his wife how clever he had been in fiddling the figures to make it look as though he was making a smaller profit than he actually was. On another occasion Andrew saw his mother pick up three pairs of tights in a department store, but when she took them to the assistant to pay for them, the girl mistakenly charged her for only two pairs; Andrew's mother, of course, said nothing.

Now neither of these two adults believed themselves to be dishonest. The father would never dream of stealing cash from anyone, and the mother would not contemplate taking an item in a shop and slipping it into her bag without attempting to pay for it. A young child, however, cannot always register such fine distinctions.

When Andrew was a little older and attending the local junior school, he and his friends would go into the corner shop while waiting for the bus home. There they would pinch sweets from the counter while the assistant wasn't looking. To the children it was great sport and they would urge each other to become more and more daring. They even worked as a team, and the misdirection they practised would be worthy of any stage magician.

The fact that a group of schoolboys regularly stole sweets from a local shop may seem comparatively unimportant; but who knows where such behaviour can lead, particularly if they find they can easily get away with it. They will be encouraged to try more and more daring thefts and if one of them – perhaps Andrew – tries to back out of the situation, he or she is likely to be ridiculed, called a 'sissy' or ostracized by the other members of the group.

Mary was in a different position. She had always been a quiet little girl who did not find it easy to make friends. When she went to her new school at the age of eleven and found herself readily accepted by a particular group of girls in her class, she did not stop to question what they were getting up to in case they turned on her and rejected her. She began to call these girls her friends, and they would all go to the High Street together on Saturday mornings to wander round the shops.

On these Saturday outings, the other girls would dare each other to steal lipsticks and other small items of make-up. Mary knew that what they were doing was wrong and she did not want to become involved but, on the other hand, she so needed to conform that she could not find the courage to protest. Although she herself did not steal anything, she went along with the others. One day the inevitable happened and they were all caught. The police naturally assumed that Mary was just as guilty as the other girls, as she had been part of the group. Fortunately for Mary, she was not charged and was simply given a lecture by a uniformed police inspector, but she had still suffered the humiliation of the arrest and the distress of seeing her mother's shocked reaction when she was escorted home by a policewoman.

It is readily accepted that many teenagers and older children commit crimes after absorbing a stimulant such as drugs or alcohol. But there are also many other contributory factors, such as a low IQ, low self-esteem, feelings of rejection or lack of achievement in school. Another cause can be the family itself and a lack of care and involvement by the parents. Such lack of care does not have to incorporate physical abuse or deprivation, simply a failure to take an interest in what the child is doing and how he is progressing.

Discipline that is either too severe or else completely erratic does nothing for the child's feelings of security, and can lead them to seek the security of a peer group that may be involved in misdemeanours of many sorts. The situation is not helped by the fact that there is today less contact with members of the extended family, which in turn leads to insecurity on the part of the child who no longer has grandparents, aunts, uncles and cousins living round the corner. Is it just coincidence that in countries like Italy and Greece, where the extended family is still important, juvenile crime figures are very much lower than in countries such as Britain and the USA?

What can you do to help your child?

- Try not to give your child the impression that some kinds of stealing (tax evasion, etc.) are not merely permissible but are actually quite clever.
- It is vital for a child to have a sense of their own value and importance. The idea is not to make them different to their peers, but to allow them to be an individual who does not feel that they are compelled to conform.
- It is not really enough to know that your child is not coming to any physical harm. While he or she is young, parents should always know where he or she is and with whom. The child needs to be secure in the knowledge that they are interested in him and in what he or she does.
- Be on the lookout for signs of stress in the child, as these may indicate either that they are unhappy within themselves and are therefore vulnerable to being influenced by other, stronger characters, or that they are feeling the strain of being involved in an activity that they know to be wrong.
- Do what you can to boost his or her self-esteem. Praise them for their efforts and achievements, however great or small. If you think that it sounds too artificial constantly to tell them how well they are doing, try saying it to someone else when you know that your child can hear.
- If you find that they have been involved in petty thieving, let them know that, although you do not approve and they must find a way of making amends, you are on their side and will be supportive while matters are being dealt with.

Smoking

Many children are pressured into smoking by their friends at school; it seems to them to be such a sophisticated thing to do. Recent figures show that more teenage girls smoke than boys and that, by the time they reach school-leaving age, many young people are already regular smokers. Apart from the fact that a child will often believe that it makes him or her appear more grown up if they smoke, if others in their class are smoking and trying to persuade them to do so then they will have to be quite strong-minded to resist. It is, of course, not the smoking itself that will attract them, but the feeling of being 'one of the gang' and of not being thought by the others to be scared to try.

Gemma was only eleven when her mother caught her hiding with a schoolfriend at the bottom of the garden and smoking a cigarette. Asked where they had obtained the cigarettes, the friend said she had taken them from her father's packet. Gemma's parents sat down with their daughter that evening and calmly presented her with the facts about the risks to her health. They were quite taken aback when she said 'But you and Daddy both smoke and you're all right'. This was in fact true, and it made the adults stop and think. They admitted to their daughter that she was right and said that they were very lucky to have escaped any illness so far but that, being in their early 40s, they could not know what lay ahead. They had a family conference and decided that they would all stop smoking together – which they did. As Gemma's mother said, 'My husband and I have always been quite healthy but I could not bear the thought that because Gemma followed our example she might be the one to develop a terrible disease.'

What can you do if your child has begun to smoke?

- Naturally, you will point out to them all the health risks involved. It is not just a matter of whether or not they develop cancer, but many other conditions are caused directly or indirectly by smoking: heart disease, bronchitis, emphysema, other lung and throat diseases, hardening of the arteries . . . and many others. If you have a daughter you can remind her that, should she continue to smoke, she stands more chance of having difficult periods, a miscarriage, or an underweight and therefore more vulnerable baby.

- Tell them that their clothes, hair and even skin will begin to smell of stale cigarettes, as will the room in which they smoke. Although they themselves may eventually not notice it, others will.
- If children are old enough, explain that they are likely to put off any prospective boy- or girlfriends if their breath smells like an old ashtray or if their fingers become nicotine stained.
- Point out just how expensive a hobby it is and how much money they will be throwing away. The most effective way is often to add up how much they would be likely to spend on cigarettes in a year, and ask them what they would like to buy if they had that money in their hand.
- Ask your child why he or she feels the need to smoke. If, as many do, they tell you that they don't want to be the one who is 'different', and all their friends are smoking, explain that there is more status to be gained by being the one who *doesn't* smoke than by being one of the herd.

Many years ago my aunt caught her twelve-year-old son and his two friends smoking behind the shed in the garden. Instead of chastising them, she told them that it would be far better if they smoked in front of her rather than in secret. She then took them into the house, sat them on the sofa and gave each of them a black Turkish cigarette to smoke. One by one the three boys turned a shade of greenish-white and had to leave the room rather hurriedly. All of them are now in their 40s, and not one of them has smoked since!

Alcohol

We hear a great deal these days about drug abuse and glue sniffing, but drinking is actually a far more extensive problem. A recent schools survey showed that many children of 11 or 12 were drinking regularly. By the time they reach 16 or 17, a large number of young people are in fact drinking every day.

This is not always something that children will do in secret to begin with, as many families allow their sons and daughters to have a drink on special occasions from quite an early age. It is not necessary to go to extremes and ban all alcohol together, as it is not likely to do any great harm in moderation and forbidding your child to touch it is likely to make them defiant and all the more determined to drink secretly. However, it should be remembered that alcohol is addictive and that stopping is much harder than starting!

What can you do if your child is drinking?

- Perhaps you could take a look at your own drinking habits. Simply enjoying a drink is not a problem; being unable to get through the day without one certainly is. The children of parents who drink regularly (even if not to excess) are far more likely to become regular drinkers themselves.
- Make sure your child learns to treat alcohol with respect, realizing it is a drug and can be just as addictive as any other substance.
- Remind them of the temporary and long-term effects of excessive drinking. In the short term it can lead to episodes of · foolish behaviour when they might be tempted to do things they will later regret. In the long term, an excess of alcohol destroys brain cells, and leads to impaired judgment and slower reflexes. It can also, of course, lead to serious and even fatal illnesses such as malfunction of the liver or certain forms of cancer.
- Ask them why they feel the need to drink. Do they believe that they need to keep pace with their friends, or does it make them feel more confident in themselves? If it is the latter, perhaps you can find some way of helping them to develop belief in their own self-worth, so they no longer need an artificial stimulant.
- If your child persists in drinking on a regular basis, you could take more drastic action by making them watch interviews or read articles about families whose entire lives have been ruined because of the actions of someone who was drunk. This may have been a drunk driver, a football hooligan or anyone else who has temporarily lost control of themselves because of alcohol.

Drug abuse

With all the media attention given to the subject, it is natural for a child to become curious about drugs. And there is no point in deluding ourselves that they are not readily available to those who seek them. Contrary to what is commonly believed, it has been found that more children are introduced to drugs by schoolfriends or at a party than by a hardened and evil pusher.

It is a mistake to think that we don't have to tackle the subject of drugs until our children are in their teens. The tendency to experiment earlier and earlier has been recognized and it is not uncommon to find children at junior school being taught about drugs and their effects on both health and behaviour. If you know that your child has been told about the subject in school, then this is the time for you to talk to them too. But do be sure that any information you have is accurate.

It is not a bad idea to ask your child outright what he or she would do if one of their friends offered them drugs or tried to tempt them to experiment with drugs at a party. Many children do not really want to become involved but find it hard to refuse a friend. In addition, they do not want to appear frightened or foolish to their contemporaries, and so join in rather than be the odd one out. If your child has already discussed with you what he or she would do if offered the chance to take drugs and how they would get out of it, they are more likely to find the strength to refuse when the time comes. Let them know that all he has to say is: 'No thank you, I'm not interested' or something similar. They don't have to give reasons or justify themselves to anyone.

Should you suspect that your son or daughter is, in fact experimenting with drugs in any form, there are many signs you can look out for.

- The child most likely to experiment in the first place is the one who is easily bored or who has little confidence in themselves. If your child has been easily led by his or her peers in the past or is vulnerable to pressure from others of their own age, they may be led by their contemporaries to try taking drugs too. The child who smokes early is also more likely to go from cigarettes to cannabis and even from cannabis to heroin. Also susceptible is the one who has always taken every opportunity to rebel against authority, whether at home or at school.
- There are common physical symptoms you can watch out for. These include frequent changes of mood, loss of appetite, constantly bloodshot eyes and secretive behaviour. But remember that these symptoms can have other causes too, both physical

and emotional, and it would be as well to check on these before rushing in and accusing your child of drug-taking.

- You can also keep an eye open for signs of 'tools of the trade', such as tubes of foil or pieces of scorched foil, caches of razor blades, drinking straws or square folds of paper. In more extreme cases you may find hypodermic syringes and needles, although once a child has progressed to this level they are usually more adept at hiding equipment.

What can you do if you think your child is on drugs?

First of all, keep calm and make sure you aren't jumping to false conclusions. If you are convinced you are right, see whether you can persuade him or her to talk to you, telling you what they have been using and how often. If you approach them in the right way, you will probably find that they are only too ready to tell you, as recent surveys have shown that most children in the early stages of drug experimentation would dearly love to give up the habit but are too frightened to tell their parents that they have become involved. So you may be doing them an enormous favour by being the one to broach the subject.

Obviously you will want to emphasize to your son or daughter just what you feel about drug abuse in any form, but try not to over-react and start ranting and raving. This would only put more pressure on them and lead them to try to escape from this extra stress by indulging even more in the habit.

If you have any doubts at all about your ability to deal with the situation, then for your child's sake you should seek professional help from people who have been trained to deal with the physical and psychological effects of drug-taking. (See Appendix for some addresses of organizations that can help.)

Glue-sniffing

Sadly, the sniffing of glue and other solvents is increasing among children and young adults. Constant smoking, drinking or drug abuse can have serious consequences, but the very first session of glue-sniffing can be enough to cause lack of consciousness or even death. It is therefore vital that if you suspect that your child or any of their companions are indulging in the habit, you report the matter to the school, the police or the social services – not with the intention of getting anyone into trouble, but because by doing so you may well save young lives.

Although there are always exceptions, there are basically two types of child likely to experiment with glue or solvent sniffing.

- The inadequate child or the one who constantly underachieves. If he or she experiences no successes, however small, they will have no feelings of self-worth. These children are more likely to try to escape by entering that psychedelic world where they will experience hallucinations that involve fantastic colours, sensations and feelings of strength and invincibility. But such feelings are often fatal. One ten-year-old child recently jumped to his death from the 18th floor of a building, convinced he could fly.
- The child who so wants to 'belong' that they are vulnerable to peer pressure. Such vulnerability will probably have shown itself quite early on in the child's school life.

What to look for

Dramatic changes in temper or behaviour are signs of glue-sniffing, as well as physical signs of glue on the hair or skin. There may even be burn marks, boils or scars on the skin if they have come into close contact with the substance.

What can you do if you suspect your child of glue-sniffing?

- The first thing is really something you should do *before* he or she reaches the stage where they are likely to become involved. If you think that your child fits one of the two categories above (or even if you don't), you could discuss with them their feelings about solvent abuse, making sure they know precisely what the results could be. Don't be too concerned about frightening them; if it saves their life it's well worth it!
- If he or she is at school, make sure that you inform the head teacher of your suspicions. If he or she has become involved through their friends, then their parents *must* be told. This is not to get anyone into trouble, but to save them from destroying their health and their lives.
- Do what you can to boost your child's confidence in themselves. Since it is usually the inadequate child who feels the need for

such escapism, they will then be less likely to experiment in the first place.

Confidence

You will have seen from the possible problems described above that the child most at risk is the one who feels insecure or inadequate. This is the child to whom conformity and acceptance by their peers are desperately important. Of course, if he or she happens to become friendly with a group of children who never go near alcohol or tobacco, there will not be a problem. But the fact is that the child who feels inadequate will want to become part of that group which is likely to consist of the more flamboyant troublemakers; it is as though he or she tries to live vicariously through these people, whom they see as everything they themselves are not.

If, from the time he or she is very young, you are able to boost your child's confidence in themselves and their abilities, you will be giving them the best possible protection against unfortunate influence. And it does not matter whether your child is academic or not; each of us has some area in which we are worthy of praise. Perhaps your son or daughter draws delightful pictures, sings sweetly or runs fast. Perhaps he or she is a kind and loving person. Whatever it is, there is always some aspect about which they have every right to feel that they are special and an achiever. Showing them that you admire this aspect will give them confidence in themselves and allow them to have a solid view of their own self-worth.

Pressure from the media

Television, videos, magazines, newspapers – all these have much to answer for when it comes to the stress they put upon our children. They put forward an image of family life bearing little resemblance to reality, but the child absorbs this image from a very early age and, when his or her own family life fails to live up to this ideal, they may feel that they are missing out on something; this in turn can cause stress.

Because the television is often right in the centre of the home – and because in many homes it is on for much of the day – it is difficult for a child to escape its influence. Even when their attention is not focused on it, they will often be subconsciously absorbing what is portrayed; in fact, this is just what makers of commercials rely upon!

Television commercials naturally tend to show 'ideal' families consisting of a father, a mother, two or three children and a pet. This immediately puts extra pressure on an only child or one who comes from a single-parent family. We have already seen that children do not like to be different, and commercials will often make them feel so. And of course the sun does not always shine, people are not always happy, parents are not always unharassed. Many families are not fortunate enough to gaze out of their window on to an expanse of well-kept garden while mother places dish after dish of delicious aromatic food on the table – and yoghurt pots don't sing and dance each time you open the fridge! While a child can make the distinction on a logical level between what is real and what is fantasy, none the less subconsciously they may grow resentful that life is not like these lovely pictures constantly placed before him or her. It is when they find that they cannot cope with the reality of life that they are likely to escape into a fantasy world of another sort; perhaps one brought about by alcohol or drugs, which induce a state of temporary euphoria.

Commercials on television and at the cinema also regularly portray images of material objects, often very expensive ones, which the child is led to believe are essential to life. And when you consider how many adults are susceptible to such advertising, is it any wonder that children are particularly vulnerable, especially when they are led to believe that everyone else has whatever item is being featured and that they must own it too to conform and to be one of the 'in crowd'.

There are many possible outcomes of over-exposure to such media pressure. Sometimes parents will over-stretch themselves financially to give in to their son or daughter who is demanding the latest toy to be shown on the screen. Obviously this is not good for the parents, but neither is it good for the child, who will simply grow up to believe that he or she must always have the latest material goody at whatever cost. Sometimes a child will actually be tempted to steal; not necessarily the item itself, but either the money with which to buy it or some other object with which they can console themselves.

If your child is not to become stressed by such propaganda at the heart of his or her own home, it is vital to realize just how intrusive television has become in the life of the average family. Naturally I am not suggesting that it should be banned, as it has many excellent aspects; simply that it should only be a *part* of daily life and should not be allowed to dominate it.

It is not only commercials that can cause problems, but the programmes themselves. An overdose of violence, sex or bad language simply makes one – adult or child – immune to the shock factor and such behaviour soon appears to be normal. We have only to think of the films of the 1940s and 1950s, in which it was customary for all the heroes and heroines to smoke – indeed it was taken as a sign of sophistication. As such it was copied by young people all over the world who were only too ready to mimic the actions of the stars. This, of course, was before the devastating effects of smoking were realized and understood, but it proves the fact that young people have always been ready to emulate what is shown on the screen.

Scenes of violence in films, videos, newspapers and on television can cause very real stress and distress to a sensitive child. This does not only apply to cowboy or war films, or even 'video nasties'. More and more distressing images are thrust at us as part of the daily news, and this may greatly upset a sensitive child. Although they cannot be shielded from all facts of life, and need to grow up knowing what is going on in the world around them – particularly if one day they are to help to change it – it is still up to the caring adult to monitor the effects of such programmes upon the child.

While no-one wishes to return to the era of Victorian prudity, much stress is caused to both boys and girls by the easy availability (indeed, brought into the home by certain daily newspapers) of titillating or pornographic material. Many a young girl is made to feel inadequate because her looks and proportions do not measure up to those of the models depicted. Many boys, seeing such images constantly before them (and it does not really make any difference if it is on the *top* shelf at the newsagent) begin to have the wrong impression of women and how they should be treated. The situation is unlikely to change and the availability of such material is unlikely to grow less, so it is up to the parents to help their children to grow up with proper perspective.

So much pressure is placed upon children by various forms of the media and by their peers that it is vital for them to feel secure in their own background if they are to resist the stress that can be caused. Such security can only be given to them by loving and caring adults who help them to grow up with a sense of their own value and a belief in themselves. This takes time, effort and an ability to communicate on the part of the adults and, although nowadays time is a truly precious commodity, giving it to your child, listening to their worries and reassuring them where necessary can reap the precious dividend of seeing them grow into a strong and secure adult with confidence in themselves and their own abilities.

7

Dealing with Common Behaviour Problems

Although it is natural for all parents to feel completely alone when their child has a particular behaviour problem, there is really nothing new in the world and every difficulty has been faced by many families in the past, is affecting many now and is bound to confront many families in the future.

Stress is involved in many, if not all, of the more common of a child's behavioural problems. His or her attitude may come about as a result of one or more of the pressures discussed already. Even if this is not the case, his or her actions and their effects upon his or her own life as well as that of those closest to them may bring about their own symptoms of stress. Naturally no child can be expected to behave perfectly at all times – indeed, I do not know of any adult who could achieve such perfection – so it is up to the individual parents to decide when their child's attitudes or actions traverse the bounds of what can be permitted, excused or tolerated. Having made this decision, the parent then has to deal with the situation as effectively as possible.

What follow are some of the more common behaviour faults of children, from the comparatively minor to the more serious, together with some suggestions as to how the varying situations may be dealt with.

Disobedience

There are many reasons why a child may be persistently and deliberately disobedient.

- Perhaps you are expecting too much of them at too early an age. It is better to have a few rules of behaviour to which the child is expected to adhere than to be excessively strict about every aspect of daily life.

- If the child is still very young, he or she may easily be carried away by the excitement of a particular occasion.
- Some children (young teenagers in particular) look on instances of deliberate disobedience as opportunities to assert their individuality.

What can you do?

- Keep the number of rules imposed to a minimum and, provided the child is old enough to understand, explain to him or her the reason for these rules and for your insistence on his or her adherence to them. Even when the child is too young to understand the reason, they should be taught to respond to the word 'no' for their own protection. How else are you to prevent them putting their finger into a live electrical socket, or pulling at the corner of a tablecloth and possibly bringing a pot of boiling water down on their head?

Use of bad language

Both boys and girls often go through a phase of using bad language.

- It may make them feel more grown-up, particularly if they are often in a situation where adults around them are using it.
- If they hear their friends swearing, they are more likely to do so too – after all, as we have already seen, children like to conform and to fit in with their peers.
- With the increase in the amount of bad language used on television and in films, the child may be imitating the behaviour of their favourite screen personality.

What can you do?

- Make it perfectly clear to your child that you will not permit bad language in your home or your company. There is little point in forbidding them to use it on any occasion, as this is likely to make it even more exciting to do so when they know they are out of earshot. Perhaps you could tell them that they will be punished by the withdrawal of privileges should they break your rule of behaviour, and that they won't be allowed to watch a favourite television programme or stay up as late as usual.

- Remember that you have to stick to your own rules! There is absolutely no point in insisting that your child does not use bad language if you do so yourself. If you expect him or her to conform to your standards, then no matter how furious or upset you may be, you must not use words you would not wish to hear them utter.

Moodiness

Moodiness can have more than one cause.

- The cause could be physical. Perhaps your child is sickening for a bout of 'flu (or has not completely recovered from one); perhaps they have had too many late nights recently.

- It is more commonly linked in some way to stress. This could be brought about by anxiety because of impending examinations, a quarrel with a schoolfriend, or a general lack of self-confidence.

What can you do?
- Arrange for a physical check-up to confirm that there is no health problem involved.
- Make sure that your child is getting enough sleep, particularly if they have a tendency to read until the early hours or if there is a television in their bedroom.
- Be understanding and make allowances for anything that may have caused additional stress, such as moving home, changing school, family problems, etc.
- Try to persuade your child to talk about how they are feeling, although never try to force the issue as this may make them withdraw even more.
- Be as patient with your child as you can. Spells of moodiness often pass of their own accord and irritation on your part could even prolong them.

Defiance

Although outright defiance may often seem like naughtiness or disobedience, there is often a deeper reason behind it. In many cases it is the child's instinctive reaction to a stressful situation.

- Perhaps your child does not fully understand what you want of them, and the confusion causes stress and anxiety.
- He or she may be reacting to what they feel are an excessive number of rules and expectations.
- As they grow, all children will test the boundaries of their freedom, always seeking a little more independence.

What can you do?

- Keep rules to a minimum and, where possible and if the child is old enough, explain the reasons for them. But, having done that, you must always insist that the rules which do exist are obeyed.
- Try not to allow yourself to become involved in pointless arguments with a defiant child – this will only cause both of you to become increasingly stressed. Once you have told them what you want, ignore their objections and act as if they had simply agreed to comply. You may find that this makes your child seem even more defiant at first but they will, in fact, be testing you to see that you mean what you say. Persist and you will find that the defiance will grow less.
- Within the bounds of common sense, allow children a little more freedom as they grow older. They will see this as a demonstration of your trust in them and, provided they understand the limitations, will be likely to behave responsibly.

Clumsiness

Excessive clumsiness may be due to some physical condition, such as poor eyesight or a problem with coordination, but if you have checked that this is not so for your child then it probably results from one of the following.

- Stress and tension: does your child appear to be worse in a stressful situation, such as when being observed by someone in authority or when they are trying particularly hard *not* to be clumsy?
- Your child may simply be one of those who does everything

hurriedly and without giving themselves time to think; but this tendency is likely to have already made itself evident in several areas of their life.

What can you do?

- If you feel that clumsiness is a reaction to anxiety or stressful situations, try not to draw too much attention to it. At the same time, see if you can find ways to increase your child's general confidence.
- If your child is one who does everything at high speed, see if you can encourage them to slow down and think before they act.
- Any child will be helped by learning a skill that involves mind and body coordination, such as dancing, gymnastics or yoga.

Untidiness

A certain amount of untidiness in child or adult is not really a problem – after all, many of us are happier when surrounded by a little clutter. But many children get to the stage where their bedrooms resemble a jumble sale before the goods have been sorted; this is not good for them physically (it is impossible for such areas to be clean) or mentally as it is extremely difficult to think clearly in the middle of chaos.

What can you do?

- Start them young! Even a toddler can be taught to put all their toys into a big box at the end of the day.
- Make sure that he or she has sufficient space in which to put their things. Allow them to choose where things are kept and then encourage them to put everything back in its place before going to bed at night.
- Set a good example. There is no point in expecting your child to be tidy if you live in a constant muddle.
- Remind him or her that it is far harder to begin to make order out of chaos than it is to put away a few things once a day.
- Once they are old enough to be able to tidy their room, never, *never*, NEVER do it for them. Many children know that if they leave their possessions in a heap for long enough, a houseproud mother is going to reach the end of her tether, and come along

97

and clear up for them. Hard as it may, just shut the door and leave them to get on with it or they will never change.

Laziness

Be sure that your child really is being lazy before you rush to criticize. Some children – just like some adults – are either brighter or more efficient than others, and may seem to be putting in less effort than the child who is less organized.

What can you do?

- Idleness is often due to a lack of motivation. The child cannot see the purpose of what they are supposed to do, whether it is a task for their mother or studying a boring subject at school. If they understand the reason for the task, or if the subject can be related to real life, they are more likely to make some effort. Perhaps they could be shown how a knowledge of mathematics can be of help in many situations, from managing accounts to piloting an aeroplane – always concentrating on their own interests.

Irresponsibility with money

Some children seem to go through all their pocket money in a day or two and then have to rely on kind (though not always wise) parents to subsidize them for the rest of the week. Not only is this unfair in childhood, it does not augur well for the future adult, who will never be able to manage his or her finances, but will always assume that someone will be there to bail them out.

What can you do?

- Allow your child to have as much practical experience as possible of handling money. Perhaps they could accompany you on shopping trips to see how much things cost.
- From as early as possible, they should be allowed to have pocket money of their own and encouraged to save a small proportion each week towards such things as holidays, birthday presents or the purchase of larger items.

- Older children can be given an allowance for out-of-school clothes, soaps, make-up, and so on.
- For holidays, give your child an allowance rather than letting them think that your purse is a bottomless pit enabling you to fund every treat. Make it clear from the very beginning that, once this money has run out, you will not be prepared to finance further. And stick to what you say!

Stealing

Always take any form of stealing seriously, even if the value of the goods taken is negligible. Physical punishment or humiliation in front of friends rarely brings about a solution to this problem, which can arise for many reasons.

- A reaction against excessively strict parental demands. The child who is never allowed to eat chocolate is quite likely to steal some from their friends should the opportunity arise.
- Envy of what others may possess, or even of what advertisements lead them to believe that others possess.
- A feeling that they aren't loved, leading them to steal things for their own comfort or to 'buy' the appreciation of others.
- A desire to conform with a group of their peers who may already be involved in theft.

What can you do?

- Make sure that he or she understands that stealing is something you will not tolerate but, having done this, encourage them to make amends by returning or replacing the stolen items. If necessary cut down their pocket money until the item has been paid for.
- Talk to your child and see if, between you, you can discover what made them steal in the first place. That way you may be able to help them overcome the basic problem.

Invasion of your privacy

Everybody, adult and child, deserves a certain amount of privacy in their lives and such privacy should always be respected. But, if you do not take the time to teach a child that there are times when you do not wish to be disturbed unless there is a real emergency and places where he or she does not enter unless requested to do so, how are they ever to learn? There are simple rules that could be accepted.

- The child should know that they don't enter their parents' bedroom without knocking or unless asked to do so.
- Handbags, diaries and wallets are personal and private, and should never be examined by anyone but the owner.
- If you decide that a specific time is yours alone – perhaps you like a relaxing bath when you come home from work, or perhaps you want to practise meditation for ten minutes a day – that wish should be respected unless an emergency arises.

What can you do?

- Make your wishes clear to your child and then ensure that these rules are always adhered to.
- Give them plenty of attention at other times so that they do not feel they are being excluded from a large part of your life.
- Allow your child to have their privacy too. If you don't want them to examine the contents of your bedroom cupboard or read your diary, then you should be willing to set them a good example by refraining from examining theirs.

Interest in pornography

It is quite normal for children, particularly after puberty, to be curious about sexual behaviour. Many adolescents are fascinated by pornographic magazines – and the fact that they are forbidden will also arouse the curiosity of younger children, particularly if they are led on by older ones. It is also quite normal for parents – particularly mothers – to be shocked and upset to discover that their child is interested in such material.

What can you do?

- Obviously how you react will depend a great deal on your own upbringing, but expressions of horror and outrage are likely to give the magazines the glamour of forbidden fruit. Forbidding your child to look at them again will merely make them all the more determined to do so in secret.

- Try and explain to your child why the fact that he or she is looking at sexually explicit magazines distresses you, and the difference between what such periodicals say about the man/woman relationship and what it is in reality.
- While making them aware of how you feel, don't let them feel guilty about their growing interest in sexual matters.

Eating problems

Problems to do with eating habits are often a symptom of excessive stress.

- The child who eats to excess may be compensating for what he or she sees as a lack of love and affection from other people, or they may be compensating for the fact that they don't like themselves very much.
- Finicky eating, or a refusal to eat at all, is often a demand for parental attention in a child who feels it is better to be noticed in a critical way than not at all.
- Although known as the 'slimmers' disease', anorexia nervosa is rarely due simply to the desire to lose weight. As with bulimia (where the sufferer will alternately diet and make themselves vomit), psychological problems generally play a large part. The sufferer is typically a girl who is young for her age, is sexually immature, and is shy and reserved, having few real friends.

What can you do?
- If your child is over-eating to a noticeable degree, see if you can discover whether he or she has any problems or worries they aren't telling you about. Perhaps they don't feel 'as good' as others; perhaps children at school have been making fun of them for some reason. Sometimes one child in a large family will feel that they are liked or loved less than his or her brothers or sisters. Even if this is not so, the effect will often be to make them compensate by overindulging in food; food representing love, warmth and nurturing.
- Should your child eat very little or be extremely fussy or faddy

101

about their food, the first thing you will naturally want to do is reassure yourself that there is no physical digestive problem or allergy that might be the cause. Once any physical cause is ruled out, perhaps you could ask yourself why your child feels the need to seek attention. Try spending a little more time simply being with them and talking to them – and yes, I know that time is hard to come by, but the resulting improvements in your child's peace of mind and state of health will make the effort well worth while. It is never a good idea to make too much fuss about the amount actually eaten or left on the plate, as this is giving them the wrong sort of attention and not helping to overcome the basic problem. A child who is not suffering from any health problem is not going voluntarily to starve themselves, so forget what your mother told you about finishing everything on your plate, and simply remove the uneaten food. But don't go and spoil things by allowing them to have sweets, crisps or biscuits afterwards. If you don't allow them anything to eat until the next meal, they will be more likely to eat well then.

- Since anorexia most commonly arises in teenage girls who have some deep underlying fear about becoming adult and coping in the grown-up world, prevention is much better than cure. As soon as your daughter reaches puberty (or even before), encourage her to talk to you about her hopes and doubts about her future and what she would like to achieve in life. Girls of this age who find no difficulty in talking to their mothers (or another caring adult woman) rarely experience the miseries of either anorexia or bulimia nervosa. Should you suspect, however, that your child is suffering from one of these two diseases, then professional help should be sought immediately as the condition left to itself can prove fatal. (See Appendix for some useful addresses.)

There are two really important ways you can help your child to avoid or overcome behavioural problems.

- Give them your time and your attention, not simply when there is some major issue to discuss but on a regular basis. If, as many children do, they always seem to demand your attention when you are particularly busy with something else, there is no harm in explaining to them that this is an inappropriate moment but that you will talk to them as soon as you have finished what you are doing. But you have to mean what you say and to keep your promise. Once they realize that you are willing to give them your undivided attention when you say you will, they won't be resentful if asked to wait. It is only when an adult is always saying 'later', but 'later' never comes, that a child's confidence in that adult is shattered.

- From the moment they are able to understand you, try and make your child believe that they are an important person in their own right. Naturally they won't be good at everything, but there is no-one who does not have some talents and aptitudes. If you can help them to believe in what they can do, and to cope with what they can't, your child will grow up having confidence and a strong self-image – essential attributes in today's stressful world.

PART THREE
How To Stress-proof Your Child

8
Stress-proofing Your Child

The title of this chapter is probably somewhat misleading, as there is no way in which you can totally stress-proof anyone, child or adult. Indeed, it would not be a good thing to do, as we need a certain amount of stress in our lives to enable us to be quick-witted, to react swiftly in situations of emergency and to come up with innovative ideas. It is not so much protecting your child from *all* stress as protecting them from *excess* stress – and you will have seen in Part One just how much damage that can do to the child's physical, mental and emotional well-being.

It is a natural instinct of a parent or other adult who has caring responsibility for a child to want to protect their charge from pain and distress, but of course this is not always possible. A combination of human frailties and outside influences will make it inevitable that your child is placed in various stressful situations as they grow up. We have already dealt with ways you can help them overcome the problems caused by particular situations, but this section of the book is devoted to ways in which you can provide your child with as sound and resilient a background as possible so that, when those stressful occasions do arise, they are more able to cope with them efficiently, making any problems less likely to cause them to suffer any long-term ill effects.

As you read the following sections, don't throw up your hands in horror and insist that there is no way in which you can put these ideas into action. Of course you can't – and it is not intended that you should. It is an ideal situation that is described; I am not expecting to make a super-human being out of you, any more than I am capable of being such a paragon myself. But if, as you read, you feel there are certain ideas you can easily incorporate into your present lifestyle without having to instigate too many dramatic changes, then perhaps you will be encouraged to do so. As for the rest, possibly you can make some of the changes suggested in a gradual way so that no great issue is made of them. And, should you suspect that your child is particularly vulnerable to stress, perhaps you could go out of your way to see what you can do to help.

Use this section of the book in whatever way you think best. As you quietly and gently make the necessary alterations in your lifestyle, you can feel secure in the knowledge that you are doing what you can to give your son or daughter a stable and secure childhood that will enable the future adult to be someone who is healthy in mind, body and spirit.

Nutrition

You will not always be in a position to do anything about the stressful situations your child may encounter, but there is one area of care where you can definitely help. You can control a great deal of what your child eats and drinks. Naturally, you can't be with them at all times supervising every morsel, but, particularly while they are very young, you can see that what they get at home is predominantly a balanced and healthy diet.

Now no-one is suggesting that you should even try to impose an impossibly strict dietary régime on a child. Indeed such an attempt would be counterproductive, as it would encourage them to rebel and to find other ways of obtaining all those goodies not permitted at home. Forget the fact that they may indulge in junk food in the school playground or when out with friends. If you can provide them with a healthy diet, rich in the correct vitamins and minerals, then the other things won't matter. In addition, if they are brought up from the very beginning to enjoy lots of fruit and vegetables and as much fresh food as possible, they are far less likely to develop a taste for sugary or fatty items.

You may wonder why, when we are trying to minimize the stress in your child's life, we are even bothering to consider what they eat and drink. It is an accepted medical fact that the person whose diet is basically healthy is far more able to withstand the physical effects of excessive stress. So, not only will you be doing what you can to improve your child's general physical health, but you will be helping them to avoid the ill effects that can be caused by outside pressures.

Suppose your family's diet to date has been less than ideal? Don't worry; it is never too late to begin to make changes. And those changes do not have to be drastic ones – those are likely to bring about screams of outrage from those who cannot understand why they are suddenly being deprived of all their favourite foods. You can make small, gradual changes in ways that interfere as little as possible with the way in which you would all choose to eat.

It is often quite difficult for an adult to judge whether or not their child is suffering from vitamin or mineral deficiency, but there are a few common symptoms that would be easy to spot. If any of these apply to your child, it might be a good idea, in addition to regulating their diet, to give them supplements in the form of tablets or capsules. The most common symptoms of vitamin or mineral deficiency are:

ridges or white flecks on the fingernails;
dull, dry hair;
tendency to mouth ulcers and bleeding gums;
dry, flaky skin;
dry skin at corners of mouth;
slow healing processes;
bruising easily;
lack of energy.

Changes you can make

- Buy *local* fresh foods where possible. All food has its highest nutritional level when just harvested.
- Use less fat by spreading butter, margarine or low-fat spread more thinly. Avoid putting butter on vegetables and try to restrict the amount of frying you do.
- Cut down on meat intake, sticking where possible to the leaner cuts, preferably white meat with the skin and all visible fat removed. Use the grill instead of the frying pan and avoid meat pies and tinned meat products.
- Eat more fish. If you must have fish in batter, buy those products that can be grilled or oven-baked rather than fried – but it is best to avoid batter altogether.
- Increase the amount of wholemeal or wholegrain bread you eat, and avoid white bread, pastry and products made with white flour. Substitute wholemeal products where you can. Choose a wholegrain cereal, and sweeten it with honey or fresh fruit rather than sugar.
- Keep cakes and biscuits for special occasions rather than having them every day.

- Use as little salt as possible when cooking – try using lemon juice or herbs instead. If you must use salt, natural sea salt is best for you. Don't encourage your child to think that they must add salt to whatever is on their plate.
- Pure fruit juices are better than fruit squashes and other soft drinks, which often have very high levels of colourings and preservatives. Skimmed milk contains less fat than other varieties and spring water or filtered water is less harmful than water straight from the tap.
- If you like tinned fruit, change to a brand that is canned in its own juice rather than in a sugar syrup. Buy low-sugar jams or honey instead of jam with a high sugar content.
- Choose wholemeal pasta rather than plain and brown rice instead of white.
- Start reading labels, so you can decide which foods are particularly high in preservatives, colouring and harmful additives and avoid them.
- Encourage your child to eat slowly, and make mealtimes a relaxing experience for them

You will see that none of the above suggestions are drastic or call for a dramatic change in your eating habits, and you don't have to try and incorporate all of them into your family diet at once. Nor should you feel guilty every time you or your child go to a birthday party or a restaurant and eat all the 'wrong' things. Nothing you eat on a special occasion will do you any great harm provided your normal everyday diet is healthy and nutritious.

Vitamins and minerals

However good your intentions, you may well have to contend with a child who is particularly fussy and faddy about what he or she eats, and although your aim should be gradually to change this state of affairs, you do have to feed them in the meantime. Also, of course, there are children who have certain allergies and therefore cannot eat a particular range of goods. In such cases the only satisfactory answer is to provide a substitute by way of a vitamin or mineral supplement.

Listed below are basic vitamins, minerals and trace elements essential to healthy growth and development – as well as to helping your child to resist the effects of stress. The foods in which they are found and the most common symptoms of deficiency are also shown.

VITAMINS

Vitamin A (carotene)

Found in green vegetables, liver, kidney, milk, cream and cheese. Deficiency symptoms include bronchial complaints, excessive catarrh and low resistance to infection.

Vitamin B_1 (thiamine)

Found in green vegetables, milk, eggs, meat, liver, yeast and wheatgerm. Deficiency symptoms include skin and hair problems, ulcers, nervous disorders, depression and blood disorders.

Vitamin B_2 (riboflavine)

Found in green vegetables, milk, eggs, meat, poultry, yeast and peanuts. Deficiency symptoms include dry hair and skin, lack of stamina, mouth ulcers, nervous disorders and poor vision.

Vitamin B_3 (pantothenic acid)

Found in brown rice, bran, liver, yeast, eggs and wholegrain products. Deficiency symptoms include dry hair and skin.

Vitamin B_6 (pyridoxine)

Found in milk, egg yolk, fish, yeast, wheatgerm, melon and cabbage. Deficiency symptoms include spots and rashes, insomnia, irritability and muscle cramps.

Vitamin B_{12} (cyanocobalamine)

Found in eggs, liver, meat, spinach, lettuce and yeast. Deficiency symptoms include anaemia, extreme tiredness, lack of appetite and skin problems.

Vitamin C (ascorbic acid)

Found in citrus fruit, raw vegetables, berries, tomatoes and melon. Deficiency symptoms include poor immunity to infection, sore or bleeding gums and pains in joints.

Vitamin D

Found in milk, butter, fish, eggs and green vegetables. Deficiency symptoms include tooth decay, calcium deficiency and bone deformity.

Vitamin E (tocopherol)

Found in milk, egg yolk, green vegetables and seed germ oils. Deficiency symptoms include muscular and nervous disorders.

Vitamin F (fatty acids)

Found in corn oil and soya products. Deficiency symptoms include brittle hair and nails, and excessive dandruff.

Vitamin K

Found in leafy green vegetables, vegetable oil, soya beans, liver and tomatoes. Deficiency symptoms include excessive bleeding from wounds and difficulty in blood clotting.

Biotin

Found in vegetables, nuts, kidney and liver. Deficiency symptoms include constant tiredness and poor skin.

Choline

Found in egg yolk, liver, dried yeast, and kidney. Deficiency causes a build-up of fatty acids in the body.

Folic acid

Found in liver, brewer's yeast and leafy green vegetables. Deficiency symptoms include anaemia.

PABA (para-aminobenzoic acid)

Found in liver, yeast, wheatgerm and molasses. Deficiency symptoms include constipation, fatigue, irritability and depression.

Inositol

Found in eggs, meat, liver, kidney, and wholegrain products. Deficiency causes a build-up of fatty acids in the body.

Niacin

Found in milk, liver, kidney, yeast and wholegrain products. Deficiency symptoms include intestinal disorders, insomnia, headaches and skin disorders.

MINERALS AND TRACE ELEMENTS

Cobalt

Found in liver, kidney and milk. Deficiency symptoms include pernicious anaemia.

Copper

Found in leafy green vegetables, liver and wholegrain products. Deficiency symptoms include general weakness and fatigue, and sores on skin.

Iodine

Found in plant and animal seafoods. Deficiency symptoms include loss of energy, dry skin and hair, and enlargement of thyroid gland.

Iron

Found in leafy green vegetables, liver, dried apricots and walnuts. Deficiency symptoms include constipation, general weakness and anaemia.

Zinc

Found in wheat bran, wheatgerm and brewer's yeast. Deficiency symptoms include delayed sexual maturity and retarded growth.

Calcium

Found in milk, dairy products and bone meal. Deficiency symptoms include brittle or soft bones, weak teeth, and pains in back and legs.

Chlorine

Found in sea salt. Deficiency symptoms include poor digestion, and weak hair and teeth.

Magnesium

Found in green vegetables, apples, almonds, corn and soya beans. Deficiency symptoms include nervousness and trembling.

Phosphorus

Found in eggs, fish, poultry, meat, nuts and wholegrain products. Deficiency symptoms include poor appetite and weight loss.

Potassium

Found in leafy green vegetables, oranges, potato skins and wholegrain products. Deficiency symptoms include heart and respiratory problems.

Sodium

Found in sea foods, sea salt, kelp, meat and beets. Deficiency symptoms include nausea, loss of appetite and weakness in muscles.

Sulphur

Found in eggs, fish, nuts, meat, cabbage and sprouts. Deficiency symptoms include poor formation of body tissue.

There is also a wide range of foods that are easily available and that will help prevent symptoms of stress in your child. Try to ensure that his or her diet contains as many of these as possible:

leafy green vegetables;
fresh fruit;
dried fruit;
soya products;
wheatgerm;
low-fat dairy food (such as low-fat yoghurt or cottage cheese).

All these are easily obtainable, easy to digest and pleasant-tasting, and can be introduced into your child's regular diet from a very early age.

Sleep

Good, sound sleep is the most natural form of healing for both mind

114

and body. But as soon as someone becomes stressed, sleep is one of the first things to suffer. This applies to children just as much as adults. You have only to think of the child who is worried about impending examinations, or even a visit to the dentist, to realize how often such anxiety is echoed by a sleepless night. And, of course, lack of sleep in itself makes the child even more tense and so it becomes harder still for them to go to sleep the following night. And so they are forced upon that exhausting and debilitating treadmill of anxiety–sleeplessness–anxiety from which it is all too difficult to escape.

It is not only the thought of something bad or frightening that can inhibit a good night's sleep. Good things cause stress too. A forthcoming birthday party or family holiday may also cause the child to have difficulty in getting to sleep, and the resulting tiredness and irritability may then spoil the anticipated occasion when it finally arrives.

You can therefore see that you can help your child considerably if you try to ensure that their normal sleep pattern is sufficient for their needs. It is not possible to specify the number of hours a child should sleep at any age because people, young and old, vary so much. A baby, of course, may sleep almost around the clock, but as the child grows they will need less sleep, although this will vary from time to time according to circumstances.

It is rarely necessary to worry about the occasional bad night, as this can happen to anyone. It is only when the isolated instance suddenly develops into a regular occurrence that you should be concerned.

It should be remembered that certain vitamin or mineral deficiencies can lead to problems in sleeping, so it would be a good idea to check your child's diet first. It may be that a simple adjustment, or even a supplement in tablet form, would be all that is needed.

You can tell whether or not your child is having sufficient sleep at night by their condition the next day. This does not mean the instant they awake – most children are extremely loath to get out of bed in the morning – but whether, after having been up for ten or fifteen minutes, they seem relatively bright and alert.

There are several things you can do to improve the situation should you believe your child is not getting enough sleep. One thing to be avoided is constant emphasis on the length and quality of their sleep. 'Did you sleep well?' 'Did you wake up in the night?' 'Are you feeling tired?' are just the sort of questions likely to cause even more stress to an already anxious child. (This emphasis on their sleeping habits and concern about their state of alertness also gives the mischievous or rebellious child a considerable amount of handy ammunition.) So play the subject down as much as possible and concentrate instead on putting into action some of the following ideas.

- Be firm about bedtime, particularly during term-time or if your child has been under the weather lately. No harm will be done if you let them stay up a little later at the weekend or during the school holidays, but don't be taken in by talk of those late television programmes that 'everybody else' is allowed to watch.
- Make their bedroom a place the child can feel relaxed and happy. If their room is somewhere they are banished to every time they misbehave, they will come to regard it with dread instead of pleasure.
- If their day has been hectic and full of activity, allow your child to have a 'winding-down' period in their bedroom before actually getting into bed. A short time spent playing with toys or looking at a book in the peace and quiet of their own room is likely to encourage them to go to sleep quickly once they do get into bed.
- It is not really a good idea for them to have a television in their bedroom as the child has yet to be born who won't be tempted to switch it on after lights out – often to see a somewhat unsuitable programme.
- Ensure that they have as much fresh air as possible during the day. It is easy to think that our children always do so, but there are many who go from home to car to school to car to home again without actually spending much time in the open air. And particularly in these days of television and video when far fewer children seem to go 'out to play', your child may be getting insufficient air and sunshine for their needs.
- Be sure, too, that they are having sufficient physical exercise each day. Most children do, in fact, have a considerable amount of exercise in school, but those who hate any form of physical education become quite adept at keeping away from the

teacher's eye and thus avoiding any really strenuous activity. But make certain that this physical exertion stops at least an hour before bedtime and that your child then indulges in some far less energetic pastime.

- Stimulating drinks can often be responsible for keeping a child awake. Remember that it is not only tea and coffee that contain caffeine or other stimulants, but also many of the sweetened or carbonated soft drinks that are so popular with children and so widely available.

- A bath just before bedtime is an excellent idea, but see that the water is neither too hot nor too cold as either of these is likely to act as a stimulant.

- Unless your child has a problem with bedwetting, a warm drink immediately before bedtime will often help him to go to sleep.

- It is good to establish a routine at bedtime, as this enables the subconscious mind to form a link between that routine and the fact of going to sleep.

- If your child reads or watches television immediately before going to bed, it could be that a little judicious censorship is called for. Obviously anything frightening or horrific can cause disturbed sleep or nightmares, but even less terrifying programmes that are none the less highly stimulating will be enough to make sleep difficult for a sensitive child.

- An older child who is concerned about their inability to get to sleep – perhaps at exam time – can be taught one of the simple relaxation techniques below. If they practise this once they are in bed, sleep will often follow naturally.

Relaxation

Many people are becoming more and more aware that learning to relax is therapeutic and beneficial. Yet somehow they never think that children need to learn to relax just as much as adults do. But, as we have seen, the modern child is subject to any number of stresses in their life, some of which are completely unavoidable. Learning how to relax can go a long way towards preventing those stresses having a detrimental effect on the child's physical, mental and emotional wellbeing.

Being relaxed does not simply mean sitting still and doing

117

nothing. Doing something you enjoy and that is far removed from whatever is causing you worry or stress is equally beneficial. Children often find that physical exertion of some sort takes their mind off their problems. Or they could find their release in any form of group activity they enjoy.

But suppose all this is not enough and your child is still exhibiting some of the symptoms of stress; what can you do? How can you help them to relax – and why should it be beneficial for them?

Just as physical changes occur in the body when we are stressed, so other physiological changes take place when we are relaxed. These include:

lowering of blood pressure;
slowing of the heart and pulse rate;
decrease in muscle tension;
decrease in flow of blood to organs and muscles;
reduction in the body's demand for oxygen;
reduction in natural output of cortisone.

The result of all these changes will be in the short term to get rid of any immediate feelings of stress and tension and to improve the general sense of wellbeing. In the long term your child will become stronger and more resilient, and therefore better able to withstand whatever stress-inducing problems fate may throw at them in the future. So learning a method of relaxation when young can provide a beneficial tool throughout life.

The younger your child is when first you start to teach them a method of relaxation, the more readily they are likely to accept it. If you think about it, what is a mother doing when she reads a story to her child after they are tucked up in bed? She is helping them to relax and to sleep well and soundly, free from childish fears and anxieties. Relaxation exercises have a similar objective and, in fact, are like stories or fantasies in themselves, as they employ that most valuable of tools – the imagination.

Teaching your child to relax
- For the very young child, telling them a ten-minute story (provided it is not too exciting) will probably suffice as a means of relaxation. They will come to associate bedtime with warmth,

love and the use of their imagination and this will stand them in good stead as they grow older.

- As the child grows, they need to be guided towards relaxation and for this they will initially need your help. Once they are in bed, ask them to tighten their muscles, making them as hard as they can, and then to allow them to become as weak and floppy as possible. They should close their eyes and listen to their own breathing, trying to establish a slow and steady rhythm. Sometimes it helps if they are encouraged to count (silently inside their head) 'one' every time they breathe in and 'two' every time they breathe out. Then you can describe a scene to them. This can be somewhere that they know and love, or it can be purely imaginary; you know your own child best and can choose something that will appeal. Indeed, you can ask them what sort of place they would like it to be. As you describe it, ask them to imagine they are actually there and can move around within that scene, looking at everything, hearing sounds and feeling whether it is warm or cold. The whole process need take no more than ten or fifteen minutes at most and it should be done immediately before the child goes to sleep. Once you have established this routine, they can be encouraged to continue for themselves, changing the scene whenever they wish to another that they find pleasant.

- The older child, of course, can have the reasons for practising a relaxation technique explained to them before being encouraged to practise it for themselves. Here more emphasis should be placed on the tensing and relaxing of each set of muscles – always starting with the feet and working upwards – and spending a few moments listening to the rhythm of their own breathing before progressing to the fantasy part of the exercise. The best time to do it is still in bed at night (after they have finished reading if that is part of the normal routine) before they go to sleep. They may need to be reminded to do it at first, but soon it can become as much of a habit as cleaning their teeth.

Positive thinking

This is something that can greatly help the child who is suffering from stress due to a particular cause. Perhaps there is an examination coming up, or maybe they have a part in the school play. It could be that they are due to compete in a race on sports day or simply that they are too nervous ever to ask a question in class. Whatever the problem, it is possible for even a very young child to learn how to use the power of their own mind to overcome it. And the technique, once learned, can be adapted and used to deal with problems throughout their life.

Let us deal with an imaginary child and an imaginary problem to see just how the technique works.

Suppose nine-year-old Alison has to perform a solo dance in a forthcoming school concert and she is becoming extremely nervous at the prospect. She is not worried about her ability to dance but about having to appear before a large audience. How will her mother help her to deal with the situation, using relaxation and positive thinking as tools?

Starting about three weeks before the actual day of the concert, Alison's mother spends about fifteen minutes with her daughter after the girl is in bed. She talks her gently through a relaxation technique as indicated above and then asks her to imagine that it is the occasion of the performance and that Alison is just about to go on stage. She asks her to imagine the scene and, while doing so, she constantly emphasizes to her daughter that she is feeling calm, relaxed and happy. Alison then has to visualize performing the dance perfectly before the audience, all of whom applaud enthusiastically when she has finished. All the time she is performing in her mind, she must be aware that she is feeling calm and relaxed.

What is Alison being encouraged by her mother to do? She is using her imagination to 'rehearse' the situation in her mind. Just as she has to rehearse the dance in reality so that she knows the steps and the movements, she can practise being in the right frame of mind. The result of the physical rehearsal will be that she will be 'movement-perfect'; the result of the mental rehearsal will be that she will be 'mind-perfect' too.

Depending on the child's age and temperament, it may be possible that you will only have to talk him or her through the situation on the first few occasions; they may be quite able to continue alone after that, and may even enjoy taking the responsibility of doing so. And, once they have seen for themselves that the technique works on one occasion, they will be able to accept that it can be adapted and used for any other.

That very simple technique can be adapted for any situation the child may encounter – and it will be equally effective in all cases. The only stipulations are that:

deliberate relaxation must come first;

they must be able to picture what it is they wish to achieve (it is no good just wanting to be 'more confident' – they must find a situation where that increase in confidence can be translated into a visual image);

belief in what they are doing is essential; they aren't wishing that something will happen, they are *making* it happen;

repetition is an essential part of the process, so they must be willing to practise it every single night for however long it takes (the ideal is to begin three weeks before the actual event).

Naturally, there are certain limitations. No amount of visualizing or positive thinking is going to perform the impossible. Brown eyes will remain brown; the smallest girl in class is not going to become the tallest. Similarly, positive thinking is used *in addition to* other things. There would be no point in Alison visualizing giving a perfect performance if she had not bothered to learn the steps of the dance. Two young athletes taking part in the same race might each visualize being the winner, but one will be physically stronger and faster than the other. However, even the one who does not win is quite likely to give the performance of their life and to do better than ever before.

By helping your child to learn positive thinking techniques you will not only be providing them with a valuable tool for the future but, because you will have to discuss the situation will them to create the correct image, you will also be encouraging them to talk to you about things that worry them.

Communication

Perhaps the most important way in which you can help your child is by talking to them, and listening to them when they talk to you. It is surprisingly easy for days or even weeks to pass with very little real communication between adult and child. Oh, there will be plenty of 'pick up your toys', 'supper's ready' and 'do turn that music down' – but that isn't what I mean by talking.

Life is very hectic today – and probably more so for parents of young children than for anyone else. They are often striving to improve their financial situation while coping with a young family. A mother may have given up her job only to find the conversation of small children somewhat limiting, or she may be trying to juggle a full-time or part-time job with running the home and caring for the family. Whatever the circumstances, time is a very valuable commodity and there is a great temptation to think that, provided your child is not being destructive and does not actually appear unhappy, then all is well. However, there is no point in waiting for symptoms of stress and anxiety to appear before you realize that perhaps they weren't so happy after all.

When is the ideal time to begin talking to your child? As soon as they are born – and certainly long before they are able to answer you! Let them know from the very beginning that your voice and the sense of your physical nearness mean security and comfort and they are far more likely to turn to you when and if problems arise later.

You cannot assume that a troubled child will seek you out and reveal their anxieties to you if you have never shown any real interest in what they are doing and thinking. And, because it is often the quietest child in the family who is the most sensitive and the most susceptible to stress, you will not always be able to guess what is going on in their mind. But if they have known for as long as they can remember that you will always find time to listen and that you are always on their side, they will eventually tell you the trouble before the problem grows too big for them to handle.

There are so many ways you can help your child.

- From the very start of their life, try and ensure that you have a 'quiet time' together every day. Even if you simply spend ten minutes with them towards the end of their day, they will come to associate that time with a feeling of such security and protection that they will be encouraged to share their hopes, fears and ideas with you.

122

- Get into the habit of talking to him or her about their day – even if they are of nursery school age. This does not mean that you have to probe like a detective, but it will let them know that you are interested in them and what they have been doing.
- Find time to do things together. A very young child may be happy to look at the pages of a picture book with you or for you to help them make a tower from bricks. The older child may prefer something more active – a walk with the dog or a visit to the local swimming pool. However you spend the time, your child will soon come to realize that this is also an ideal opportunity for conversation.
- Whatever they tell you, try not to appear shocked. For example, it is natural for small children to examine their own and each other's bodies out of curiosity, and any demonstration of shock or disgust on your part could well cause your child to think there is something terribly wrong with bodies in general and their own in particular. If an older child comes to you with details of what may amount to sexual abuse, then any expression of shock or horror could increase their sense of guilt. Even if they confess to you that they have done something wrong, it is essential that you deal with the matter as calmly and supportively as possible.
- Let your child know you are proud of them and their abilities. Whether they are top of their class in history, the best swimmer in the school or simply a kind and caring person, every child has some way that they can be considered 'special'. Remember it is equally important for them to feel that they can discuss their failures or difficulties with you too, so that you can reassure them that you understand and will do what you can to help.
- Remember that no child is born without confidence; it has to be taken away. Just like any adult, every child needs to know that they are loved and to have their belief in themselves nurtured, so they can grow up to become a person with a healthy self-image that will stand them in good stead throughout life.

Most of this book has concentrated on how to help your child overcome problems in his or her life and the stress those problems can cause. If, from the very outset, you can find the time to talk to them and to do things with them these problems are far less likely to occur in the first place. By helping them during their childhood, you will be playing your part in creating the healthy, happy adult of tomorrow. As a relaxed and confident adult, they will then be more likely to take time and trouble with their own children when the time comes. So what you do now can affect not only your child's future but the future of generations to come.

Useful Information

Divorce and separation

Conciliation services (to help sort out arrangements with regard to children)

Institute of Family Therapy
43 New Cavendish Street
London W1M 7RG

Solicitors' Family Law Association
24 Croydon Road
Keston
Kent BR2 6EJ

Books

(For younger children)
Nystrom, Carolyn *Mike's Lonely Summer* (Lion 1986)

(For older children)
Krementz, Jill *How it Feels when Parents Divorce* (Gollancz 1985)

(For adults)
Wallerstein, Judith S. and Blakeslee, Sandra *Second Chances* (Bantam 1989)

The child victim

Books
Elliott, Michele *Keeping Safe* (New English Library 1988)

Bereavement

Cruse
Cruse House
126 Sheen Road
Richmond
Surrey TW9 1UR

Compassionate Friends
6 Denmark Street
Bristol BS1 5DQ

Books
Wright, Marion *A Death in the Family* (Macdonald Optima 1987)

Problems at school

British Dyslexia Association
Church Lane
Peppard
Oxfordshire RY9 5JN

National Confederation of Parent Teacher Associations
43 Stonebridge Road
Northfield
Gravesend
Kent DA11 9DS

Behaviour

Anorexic Aid
The Priory Centre
11 Priory Road
High Wycombe
Buckinghamshire HP13 6SL

National Campaign Against Solvent Abuse
Box S15
245a Coldharbour Lane
London SW9 8RR

ASH (Action on Smoking and Health)
5–11 Mortimer Street
London W1N 7RH

Narcotics Anonymous
PO Box 417
London SW10 0DP

Families Anonymous
5–7 Parsons Green
London SW6 4UL
(Drug abuse)

Children's Legal Centre
20 Compton Terrace
London N1 2UN

General

Books

Sokolov, Ivan and Hutton, Deborah *The Parents' Book* (Thorsons 1988)

Lewis, David *Helping Your Anxious Child* (Mandarin 1989)

Index